context

a scriptural
journal
based on
the Moravian
Daily Texts

Augsburg Fortress

Context
A Scriptural Journal Based on the Moravian Daily Texts

Designer: Alan Furst
Editors: Roxann Miller, Jeffrey S. Nelson, and Julie Lindesmith

---

ISBN 0-8066-4193-2

Manufactured in the U.S.A.

03 02 01 00 99 1 2 3 4 5 6 7 8 9 10

FAQs

Give me a brief overview: What is *Context*?

Context is a devotional journal prepared by persons age 16 through 30 (approximately). It includes an Old Testament Scripture verse followed by a reference to a contemporary song; then a New Testament Scripture verse followed by a second reference to a contemporary song; and concludes with a short prayer. In addition, it presents an organized approach to daily Scripture readings and provides a place for users to express their own thoughts and reflections.

Who else is reading these texts?

Around the world there are more than 1.5 million believers using these texts on a daily basis. Versions of the *Moravian Daily Texts* are produced in more than 50 languages and dialects.

What is the best way to use this resource?

It depends on what you want to gain from your quiet time. If you're just getting started or have struggled to maintain a devotional schedule, then this is a concise, simple way to begin: Read the verses; listen to, sing, or reflect upon the songs; then pray the final prayer, adapting it as needed to fit the challenges in your life that day.

Many people also find it helpful to organize their thoughts and reflections as they meditate on God's Word. If you are among them, we invite you to journal. Journaling can also be a good way to keep track of your own spiritual growth and God's answers to prayer.

If you're looking for a deeper study, there's also a systematic approach to reading through the Psalms in one year and the entire Bible in two years.

Explain the Bible readings at the top of each day.

The Psalms reference allows users to read through the entire book of Psalms in one year. The book of Psalms is great to study because it reflects the wide range and depth of emotions that we all experience. It also illustrates God's presence and faithfulness in every situation.

The Old and New Testament references guide readers through a two-year process of reading the entire Bible in a systematic manner.

The Bible verses in the text are not in any order. How were they chosen?

The verses used in the Old Testament references (watchwords) are selected from Scriptures that were first used in *Daily Texts* prepared in the 1700s by Nicholas Ludwig von Zinzendorf. The entire collection of watchwords totals 1780 and is stored in Herrnhut, Germany. Once texts are drawn, they are set apart for three years before being reused.

The New Testament verses are intentionally selected with the particular occasion or the needs of the user in mind. Traditionally, the North American edition has added an appropriate hymn verse after each Scripture passage.

Why should I consider journaling?

Journaling can be a helpful tool in your spiritual journey. By recording your ideas, revelations, thoughts, and prayer requests on a regular basis you will begin to have a visible record of your own spiritual growth. In addition, you will be prepared to jot down the first inklings of plans for the future (before they are forgotten in the rush of daily life).

But probably one of the best reasons to journal is to develop your own stories of God's faithfulness. By keeping a record of prayer requests and recording the ways God has answered those prayers, you will be creating a personal testimony of God's ongoing love for you. That way when times are really rough, you don't have to struggle to remember that God really is good; you can simply look back at the high points in your journal.

How can I listen to these suggested songs without buying 700 CDs?

Copyright considerations prohibit us from providing all the lyrics, but hopefully we have done the next best thing. By listing the song title, artist, album, year and label we have tried to make it easy to find more information about the music. Musical clips of many of these songs are available for listening (and purchase) on web sites such as www.augsburgfortress.org, www.christianbook.com or www.cdnow.com, as well as many other sites that offer listening clips. For songs not readily available at those sources, we have listed the artist's website. In addition, if everyone in your small group is using this resource, you might be able to coordinate with others in your groups to bring the appropriate songs to your weekly meeting and play them for all to hear at that time. In developing this resource authors accessed a variety of musical forms, both Christian and mainstream with the assumption that faith might be deepened.

What are the *Moravian Daily Texts?*

The *Moravian Daily Texts* date back to 1727. After the congregation at Herrnhut, Germany, experienced a renewal experience (August 13, 1727), church leaders wanted to keep that newly rekindled fire burning. So they appointed a person to visit each home in the little community each morning. That person's task was to encourage all the other brothers and sisters "to watchfulness and faithful endurance" throughout the day. To facilitate these visits, Zinzendorf wrote out a Scripture verse or hymn stanza that seemed appropriate for the day. This became the "watchword" or theme for the day.

It was not until 1731 that the texts were chosen for a year in advance and printed in the form of a little booklet, so that year really marks the beginning of the *Moravian Daily Texts* as a publication of the church. The verses used in this journal are based on the verses for 2002.

What is the watchword?

The German word *Losung,* from which the German title of the *Daily Texts* is taken, really means a signal that is agreed upon: a password, countersign, or watchword. It is a military term, which may seem strange in light of the efforts of Moravians to live at peace with one another.

Even though the early Moravians desired to live peaceably with others, they understood that they were soldiers of Christ who warred against Satan and all his hosts. They considered the battle against sin to be a daily conflict, so their watchword was more than a theme for the day. It was the password they used in identifying themselves in the same way that a password is used in military camps.

In addition, that watchword was more than just a verse that was read in the morning. Early accounts indicate that as the watchword was discussed and its meaning applied to their own lives in various services and in casual conversations, it became apparent as to who was "one with them in spirit" and who was not.

Who are the Moravians?

The short story is that the Moravian church is one of the oldest Protestant denominations in the world, even predating the Reformation. They were the first to send out Protestant missionaries and have a strong history of ministering to native peoples. Today there are nearly 50,000 Moravians worshiping in more than 150 congregations in the United States alone. If you were to visit a Moravian congregation, you would probably find many similarities to a Lutheran congregation.

For you history buffs, here's the longer story:

The roots of the Moravian church predate the Reformation of Martin Luther by a number of decades—in 1457 to be exact—beginning in ancient Bohemia and Moravia as people followed the teachings of John Hus. The name Moravian comes from the geographic region in which they lived.

Hus was a Roman Catholic priest and professor at the University of Prague. An innovator for his time, Hus taught his students that the gospel should be available in the language of the people rather than in Latin, and that both the communion bread and wine should be freely available to all believers. He even went so far as to hold worship services in Czech and objected to abusive practices of the fifteenth century Roman Catholic church. For all of this, he was labeled a heretic and burned at the stake in 1415.

Despite his death, Hus's belief in the authority of Scripture over the church and church leadership became a cornerstone of the Reformation. But over the next 40 years, the followers of Hus found little else upon which to agree. No single leader emerged that could keep the various factions together.

Finally, in 1457, a small group broke away and established a fellowship with the goal of living in peace and following as closely as possible the example of the New Testament church. This group became known as the Unity of Brethren, or in Latin, *Unitas Fratrum*.

In spite of persecution, this group grew. Today we would probably say they were an underground church. But their faith continued, handed down from parents to children. They published the first recorded hymnal in 1501 and completed the Kralitz Bible, translated in the Czech language, between 1579 and 1593. For nearly 100 years, these believers met as small groups in homes or forest settings to sing hymns and share Scriptures, hiding their Bibles and hymnals under the floorboards of their homes for safekeeping.

In the early 1700s, a group of Moravians crossed the border into southern Germany to seek refuge and religious freedom on the estate of the Lutheran Count Nicholas Ludwig von Zinzendorf. A remarkable outpouring of the Holy Spirit came upon these believers on August 13, 1727. Petty quarrels were put aside, and the entire congregation was united with a spirit of love and power. This was soon manifested in the lives of the people by a strong desire to share Christ with those—particularly the disenfranchised—who had not had an opportunity to hear. In 1732 the first Moravian missionaries landed on St. Thomas in the Virgin Islands, bringing the gospel to the slaves of the island. Little did they know that in their obedience they were also launching the modern missionary movement of the Protestant church.

Moravian missionaries first came to what is now the state of Georgia in 1735. In 1740 they brought God's word to Native Americans in Pennsylvania, founding Bethlehem in 1741. They founded Salem (now Winston-Salem) North Carolina in 1753. Some historic buildings in Old Salem and Bethlehem are still standing—a testament to the faithfulness of these believers.

Today, Moravians continue to place a strong emphasis on education. As founding members of the World Council of Churches and the National Council of Churches, they also continue to work for Christian unity.

WEEK 1

sunday

Watchword for the Week

And the Word became flesh and lived among us, and we have seen his glory, the glory as of a father's only son, full of grace and truth. John 1:14

Sing praises to the LORD, for he has done gloriously; let this be known in all the earth. Isaiah 12:5

"Raise" by Circadian Rhythm (*Over Under Everything* ©2001, 40 Records)

[Paul said:] "If I proclaim the gospel, this gives me no ground for boasting, for an obligation is laid on me, and woe to me if I do not proclaim the gospel!" 1 Corinthians 9:16

"Invade My Soul" by By the Tree (*Invade My Soul* ©2001, Fervent Records)

Father, you should be the one who is filling our hearts, but often we give other things priority. Take the evil and impure things from our lives and help us grow in a relationship with you so you are the only thing in our hearts. Amen

WEEK 1

monday

Psalm 149
Psalm 150

I will instruct you and teach you the way you should go; I will counsel you with my eye upon you. Psalm 32:8

"Open the Eyes of My Heart" by Michael W. Smith (*Worship* ©2001 Reunion)

When he saw the crowds, he had compassion for them, because they were harassed and helpless, like sheep without a shepherd. Matthew 9:36

"Faith" by Jason Upton (*Faith* ©2001, 40 Records)

Lord, we can be so thickheaded at times. We have heard your words, yet oftentimes we refuse to pay attention. We have seen your wonderful works, yet we reject your teachings. Forgive us for our unintelligent choices. We know you not only made the universe, you command it as well. We want to follow your commands. Teach us to listen. Amen

WEEK 1

tuesday

■ Psalm 1
  Genesis 1:1—2:3; Matthew 1:1-17

...ep my statutes, and observe them; I am the LORD; I
...nctify you. Leviticus 20:8

▌ "Lead Me" by Raze (*Power* ©1999,
  EMD/Chordant)

...we live by the Spirit, let us also be guided by the
...irit. Galatians 5:25

▌ "If You Want Me To" by Ginny Owens (*A Night
  in Rocketown* ©1999, Sony/Word)

...ear Heavenly Director, let us not forget as we go
...rough the day to listen to your guidance. It is some-
...nes hard for us to remember that we do not know
...erything. Help us to keep in mind that we need to
...st in you and follow your instructions as we live
...r lives. Amen

WEEK 1

wednesday

■ Psalm 2
  Genesis 2:4-25; Matthew 1:18-25

...muel said, "To obey is better than sacrifice."
...Samuel 15:22

▌ "Running Out of Time" by Ken Holloway (*The
  Ordinary* ©Provident)

...hoever obeys [God's] word, truly in this person the
...ve of God has reached perfection. 1 John 2:5

▌ "Long Way Home" by All Weather Human (*If
  the Bough Breaks* ©All Weather Human. Lyrics
  online at ww.allweatherhuman.com/lyrics.html)

...ear Father, it is always hard to obey when we are
...re we know better. Help us to learn that obedience
... you is much more beneficial for us than reliance
... ourselves. And when we obey you, we can then
...come even closer to you. Amen

WEEK 1

■ Psalm 3
■ Genesis 3:1—4:26; Matthew 2:1-12

You show me the path of life. Psalm 16:11

> "I Am Found in You" by Steven Curtis Chapman (*Greatest Hits* ©1997, EMD/Chordant)

Simon Peter answered him, "Lord, to whom can we go? You have the words of eternal life. We have come to believe and know that you are the Holy One of God." John 6:68-69

> "Thy Word" by Amy Grant (*The Collection* ©1990, Myrrh)

Dear Heavenly Guide, we often get lost in our everyday lives. Help us to know that it is you who can show us the right path, who can lead us out of darkness. Thank you for always finding us when we cannot find you. Amen

WEEK 1

■ Psalm 4
■ Genesis 5:1-32; Matthew 2:13-23

And I will pour out a spirit of compassion and supplication on the house of David and the inhabitants of Jerusalem. Zechariah 12:10

> "What Manner of Love" by Watermark (*Watermark* ©1999, Sony/Word)

And because you are children, God has sent the Spirit of his Son into your hearts, crying, "Abba! Father!" Galatians 4:6

> "You're My Little Girl" by Go Fish (*Acappella* ©inpop/Chordant. For more information see: www.singers.com/gospel/gofish.html)

Dear Father God, we are so lucky to have you as a parent. You love us unconditionally, no matter what. Thank you for always caring for us and being there when we need you. Amen

WEEK 1

■ Psalm 5
■ Genesis 6:1—7:10; Matthew 3:1-17

[T]t the LORD God called to the man, and said to him,
[W]here are you?" He said, "I heard the sound of you
[in] the garden, and I was afraid."
[Ge]nesis 3:9-10

"Much Afraid" by Jars of Clay (*Much Afraid*
©1997, BMG/Jive/Silvertone)

[Go]d did not give us a spirit of cowardice, but rather a
[spi]rit of power and of love and of self-discipline.
[2 T]imothy 1:7

"23" by All Weather Human (*If the Bough
Breaks* ©All Weather Human. Lyrics online at
www.allweatherhuman.com/lyrics.html)

*[De]ar Lord, thank you for being there when we are
[afr]aid. Fear is never something we want to admit or
[ad]mit to, but help us to remember that it is only
[thr]ough confessing our fears to you that you can help
[us] overcome them. Amen*

WEEK 2

Watchword for the Week
The darkness is passing away and
the true light is already shining.
1 John 2:8

[Th]e LORD stirred up the spirit...of all the remnant of the
[pe]ople; and they came and worked on the house of
[the] LORD of hosts, their God. Haggai 1:14

"He Knows" by 18 Inch Journey (*Dive In* ©18
Inch Journey. For more information click on
www.18inchjourney.com)

[Th]erefore, my beloved, be steadfast, immovable,
[alw]ays excelling in the work of the Lord, because you
[kn]ow that in the Lord your labor is not in vain.
[1 C]orinthians 15:58

"I Believe the Presence" by Darlene Zschech
(*Shout to the Lord* ©1998, Sony/Word)

*[De]ar Heavenly Supporter, sometimes it is so hard to be
[a] witness for you when we don't see any results. Help
[us] to stay optimistic and focused when we are living
[for] you. Thank you for knowing all the troubles we go
[th]rough and helping us when we ask. Amen*

WEEK 2

■ Psalm 6
■ Genesis 7:11—8:22; Matthew 4:1-11

With him are strength and wisdom; the deceived and the deceiver are his. Job 12:16

> "God So Loved the World" by Jaci Velasquez (*Jaci Velasquez* ©1998, Sony/Word)

[God our Savior] desires everyone to be saved and to come to the knowledge of the truth. 1 Timothy 2:4

> "Never Be" by Carman (*Mission 3:16* ©1998, EMD/Chordant)

Dear forgiving Father, thank you for giving us all the chance to know you. Help us to always remember that everyone is loved by you and we, as Christians, need to show your love to all. Thank you for loving us unconditionally. Amen

---

WEEK 2

■ Psalm 7:1-9
■ Genesis 9:1-29; Matthew 4:12-25

Let this be recorded for a generation to come, so that a people yet unborn may praise the LORD. Psalm 102:18

> "Praise the King" by Cindy Morgan (*A Night in Rocketown* ©1999, Sony/Word)

But the tax collector, standing far off, would not even look up to heaven, but was beating his breast and saying, 'God, be merciful to me, a sinner!' Luke 18:13

> "Portrait of an Apology" by Jars of Clay (*Much Afraid* ©1997, BMG/Jive/Silvertone)

Dear heavenly Father, so often we talk to you only when we want something. We don't remember to pray to say thanks, to praise you for your goodness. We forget to confess our sins to you, in order to seek forgiveness. Help us to remember to go to you for all things. Amen

WEEK 2

Psalm 7:10-17

Genesis 10:1—11:9; Matthew 5:1-16

You are the God of my salvation; for you I wait all day long. Psalm 25:5

| "Not Home Yet" by Steven Curtis Chapman (*Greatest Hits* ©1997, EMD/Chordant)

Ask and you will receive, so that your joy may be complete. John 16:24

| "Steady On" by Point of Grace (*Steady On* ©1998, Sony/Word)

Dear Lord, waiting is one of the hardest things we can do, especially when we don't know what is going to happen. Help us to remember to trust in you and wait for your commands. Then we can enjoy life if we place our worry in your hands. Amen

WEEK 2

Psalm 8

Genesis 11:10—12:9; Matthew 5:17-26

For the LORD will vindicate his people, and have compassion on his servants. Psalm 135:14

| "Honor and Praise" by Twila Paris (*Where I Stand* ©1996, EMD/Sparrow)

Blessed are those who hunger and thirst for righteousness, for they will be filled. Matthew 5:6

| "Seek Ye First" (*WoW Worship Green* ©2001, Sony/Epic)

Dear loving Judge, so often we see those who seem to get away with evil things. It makes us wonder why we try to be good if doing the wrong thing is easier. Help us to remember that we are doing right because it pleases you and you will be the final judge of everyone. Amen

WEEK 2

■ Psalm 9:1-10
■ Genesis 12:10—13:18;
Matthew 5:27-42

Waters shall break forth in the wilderness, and
streams in the desert. Isaiah 35:6

> "He Will Make a Way" by Kathy Troccoli
> (*Corner of Eden* ©1998, Reunion)

Jesus cried out, "Let anyone who is thirsty come to
me." John 7:37

> "Don't You Know" by Go Fish (*Out of Breath*
> ©inpop/Chordant. For more information see:
> www.singers.com/gospel/gofish.html)

*Dear heavenly Inspirer, you are there even when we
sometimes think there is only emptiness. Thank you
for encouraging us in what we have to do in life.
Help us to have faith that you are there no matter
what. Amen*

WEEK 2

■ Psalm 9:11-20
■ Genesis 14:1—15:21;
Matthew 5:43—6:4

I have been pouring out my soul before the LORD.
1 Samuel 1:15

> "Take It to the Lord" by 18 Inch Journey (*Dive
> In* ©18 Inch Journey. For more information click
> on www.18inchjourney.com)

On that day you will ask nothing of me. Very truly, I
tell you, if you ask anything of the Father in my
name, he will give it to you. John 16:23

> "Power of a Moment" by Chris Rice (*Past the
> Edges* ©1998, Sony/Word)

*Dear Guiding Light, thank you for always being there
for us. So often we don't know what to do and have
so many questions that we ourselves cannot answer.
But no matter what we ask, you always answer.
Thank you. Amen*

sunday

Watchword for the Week

For all who are led by the Spirit of God are children of God. Romans 8:14

will give you as a light to the nations, that my salvaon may reach to the end of the earth. Isaiah 49:6

"Into Jesus" by dc Talk (*WoW 1999* ©1998, EMD/Chordant)

sus said to them again, "Peace be with you. As the ather has sent me, so I send you." John 20:21

"Testify to Love" by Avalon (*WoW 1999* ©1998, EMD/Chordant)

ear God, you have asked us to be a witness for you. hat sometimes feels like a job too big to handle. Not ll of us are good speakers or leaders. Help us to member that we can be a witness just by letting your ve shine through us. Amen

monday

Psalm 10:1-11
Genesis 16:1—17:27;
Matthew 6:5-18

oseph said to his brothers, "Do not quarrel along the ay." Genesis 45:24

"When I See Love" by All Weather Human (*If the Bough Breaks* ©All Weather Human. Lyrics online at www.allweatherhuman.com/lyrics.html)

or this is the message you have heard from the eginning, that we should love one another. John 3:11

"Love Me Good" by Michael W. Smith (*Live the Life* ©1998, BMG/Jive/Silvertone)

oving Father, as we get older we change and somemes our families and friends don't adapt to our new ves as quickly as we do. Help us to remember to ve them no matter what and to be patient with em as well, just as you are patient and always love s. Amen

WEEK 3

■ Psalm 10:12-18
■ Genesis 18:1-33; Matthew 6:19-34

And [the LORD spoke], "…I will be gracious to whom I will be gracious, and will show mercy on whom I will show mercy." Exodus 33:19

"Driven to Humanity" by Watermark (*Watermark* ©1999, Sony/Word)

[The landowner said to the laborers:] "I choose to give to this last the same as I give to you. Am I not allowed to do what I choose with what belongs to me? Or are you envious because I am generous?" Matthew 20:14-15

"You Are God Alone" by The Parachute Band (*Always and Forever* ©1999, Here to Him)

Dear heavenly Provider, you are gracious and generous to us, but sometimes we forget that it is you who make the decisions. Help us to remember that your will is the best for us all and lead us back on your path when we are lost. Amen

WEEK 3

■ Psalm 11
■ Genesis 19:1-29; Matthew 7:1-12

Remember the days of old, consider the years long past; ask your father, and he will inform you; your elders, and they will tell you. Deuteronomy 32:7

"I'm Alright" by Ffh (*I Want to Be Like You* ©1998, BMG/Brentwood)

Now faith is the assurance of things hoped for, the conviction of things not seen. Indeed, by faith our ancestors received approval. Hebrews 11:1-2

"Since I Met You" by dc Talk, (*Supernatural* ©1998, EMD/Virgin)

I'm OK Lord. Through faith, I know that as long as I trust in you, even when I have lost all hope, I will be all right. Help me consider my experiences and the advice of my friends to help me face everything ahead of me today. Thanks for being there, Lord. Amen

WEEK 3

thursday

- Psalm 12
- Genesis 19:30—20:18;
Matthew 7:13-23

ift up your eyes on high and see: Who created
ese? He who brings out their host and numbers
em, calling them all by name. Isaiah 40:26

"Awesome God" by Rick Mullins (*WoW Gold*
©2000, BMG/Brentwood)

y faith we understand that the worlds were prepared
y the word of God, so that what is seen was made
om things that are not visible. Hebrews 11:3

"God" by Rebecca St. James (*God* ©1996,
EMD/Chordant)

awesome God—you created so many wonderful
ings in this world. How amazing you are to have
ade me and so many other beautiful things through
ur love. Thank you for creating us and the world
e live in. Amen

WEEK 3

friday

- Psalm 13
- Genesis 21:1-34; Matthew 7:24—8:4

essed be the LORD, who has given rest to his
eople Israel according to all that he promised.
Kings 8:56

"Outro (Amazing Grace)" by Destiny's Child
(*The Writings on the Wall* ©1999,
Sony/Columbia)

nce Jesus was asked by the Pharisees when the
ngdom of God was coming, and he answered, "The
ngdom of God is not coming with things that can be
oserved; nor will they say, 'Look, here it is!' or 'There
is!' For, in fact, the kingdom of God is among you."
uke 17:20-21

"You Are My All in All" by Dennis Jernigan
(*Vol.2 You Are My All in All* ©2000, Here to
Him)

mighty God, your Son said that the kingdom of
od is among us. We know this to be true because
e can feel your power and love around us every
ay. We love to see your amazing saving grace in our
ves. Please remain with us forever. Amen

WEEK 3

▪ Psalm 14
▪ Genesis 22:1-24; Matthew 8:5-22

But let justice roll down like waters, and righteousness like an ever-flowing stream. Amos 5:24

> "Great Is the Lord" by Michael W. Smith (*First Decade 1983-93* ©1993, Reunion)

He himself bore our sins in his body on the cross, so that, free from sins, we might live for righteousness. 1 Peter 2:24

> "Live for You" by Rachael Lampa (*Live for You* ©2000, Sony/Word)

O great God, we realize how wonderful it was that Jesus died to save us from our sins. Help us to live a life of righteousness like his. Teach us also to serve you all the days of our lives. We love you, Lord. Help us live for you. Amen

WEEK 4

Watchword for the Week
The LORD will arise upon you, and his glory will appear over you. Isaiah 60:2

There is no Holy One like the LORD, no one besides you; there is no Rock like our God. 1 Samuel 2:2

> "Me without You" by Rebecca St. James (*God* ©1996, EMD/Chordant)

There is one God, the Father, from whom are all things and for whom we exist, and one Lord, Jesus Christ, through whom are all things and through whom we exist. 1 Corinthians 8:6

> "I Need You" by Leann Rimes (*I Need You* ©2001, CURB)

O magnificent Lord, you have made all things through yourself and Jesus Christ. There is no one like you. We need you Lord, for without you we are nothing. You are the only God. Please don't leave us alone. Amen

WEEK 4

Psalm 15
Genesis 23:1—24:25;
Matthew 8:23-34

[Hagar] named the LORD who spoke to her, "You
e El-roi"; for she said, "Have I really seen God and
mained alive after seeing him?" Genesis 16:13

"Sometimes by Step" by Rich Mullins (*Songs*
©1996, Reunion Records)

athanael said to Jesus, "Rabbi, you are the Son of
od! You are the King of Israel!" John 1:49

"God You Are My God" by Delirious? (*Glo*
©2000, EMD/Sparrow)

God, you are truly our God. We have seen your
ower and love through other people who love you
nd every wonder you have created. We realize that
ou really are our God and are a very important part
of our lives today. We will praise you forever! Amen

WEEK 4

Psalm 16:1-6
Genesis 24:26-66; Matthew 9:1-13

ou say, "I am innocent; surely his anger has turned
om me." Now I am bringing you to judgment for
aying, "I have not sinned." Jeremiah 2:35

"Go and Sin No More" by Rebecca St. James
(*God* ©1996, EMD/Chordant)

we say that we have no sin, we deceive ourselves,
nd the truth is not in us. 1 John 1:8

"Between You and Me" by dc Talk (*Jesus Freak*
©1995, EMD/Chordant)

ord, we confess that we are sinners. No one is with-
ut sin. We would be lying if we said that we haven't
nned. Help us to resist temptations and the peer
ressure around us. Please forgive us for all of our
ns. Thank you for your forgiveness, Lord. Amen

WEEK 4

■ **Psalm 16:7-11**
■ **Genesis 25:1-34; Matthew 9:14-26**

All the nations you have made shall come and bow down before you, O LORD, and shall glorify your name. Psalm 86:9

> "Everybody Praise" by Acappella (*Gold* ©2000, The Acappella Company)

And he said to them, "Go into all the world and proclaim the good news to the whole creation." Mark 16:15

> "Go Tell it on the Mountain" Simon & Garfunkel (*Wednesday Morning, 3 a.m.* ©1964, Sony/Columbia)

O Lord you are wonderful! We rejoice at the sound of your name. You fill every day with such joy, we want to share your majesty and love with everyone we meet! You truly are magnificent. Amen

---

WEEK 4

■ **Psalm 17:1-7**
■ **Genesis 26:1-20; Matthew 9:27-38**

With my mouth I will give great thanks to the LORD; I will praise him in the midst of the throng. Psalm 109:30

> "Sing Your Praise to the Lord" by Rich Mullins (*Songs* ©1996, Reunion)

Blessed be the God and Father of our Lord Jesus Christ, who has blessed us in Christ with every spiritual blessing in the heavenly places. Ephesians 1:3

> "Lord, I Lift Your Name on High" by Sonicflood (*Sonicpraise* ©2000, EMD/Chordant)

O amazing Lord, we want to praise you forever. You are so fantastic! Thank you for sending your Son for us. Thank you for everything you have given us, and always being there for us.

We will praise you forever. Amen Lord!

WEEK 4

Psalm 17:8-15
Genesis 26:21—27:29;
Matthew 10:1-16

This poor soul cried, and was heard by the LORD, and was saved from every trouble. Psalm 34:6

"I Am the Way" by Mark Schultz (*Mark Schultz* ©2000, Sony/Word)

If you keep my commandments, you will abide in my love, just as I have kept my Father's commandments and abide in his love. I have said these things to you so that my joy may be in you, and that your joy may be complete. John 15:10-11

"It's Been a Long Time" by Ffh (*Found a Place* ©2000, Reunion)

Help us O God. We look to find our joy in you. Please hear our cry and be with us through our many times of trouble. We know that all we have to do is call you and you will be there for us. Please be there for us forever. Amen

WEEK 4

saturday

Psalm 18:1-6
Genesis 27:30—28:9;
Matthew 10:17-26

You shall be called priests of the LORD, you shall be named ministers of our God. Isaiah 61:6

"It's Alright (Send Me)" by Winans Phase2 (*We Got Next* ©1999, Sony/Word)

Jesus Christ, the faithful witness, first born of the dead, and ruler of the kings of the earth. To him who loves us and freed us from our sins by his blood, and made us to be a kingdom, priests serving his God and Father, to him be glory and dominion forever and ever. Amen. Revelation 1:5-6

"Hands and Feet" by Audio Adrenaline (*Underdog* ©1999, EMD/Chordant)

O God, to be a messenger of your love is so awesome. At this point in our lives, we may feel like we don't really know how. Teach us to be your servants. Let us be your hands and your feet. We will serve you today and every day of our lives. Amen

WEEK 5

sunday

Watchword for the Week
We do not present our supplication before you on the ground of our righteousness, but on the ground of your great mercies. Daniel 9:18

God blessed them, and God said to them, "Be fruitful and multiply, and fill the earth and subdue it." Genesis 1:28

> "This Good Day" by Fernando Ortega (*Home* ©2000, Sony/Word)

All belong to you, and you belong to Christ, and Christ belongs to God. 1 Corinthians 3:22-23

> "Because of Who You Are" by Ffh (*A Place* ©2000, Reunion)

Great Creator, you give so many great and beautiful gifts every day. We will try to care for all that you have created. All of your wonderful creatures are great and we know that you are the magnificent one who has created them. Thank you for creating our world! Amen

WEEK 5

monday

■ Psalm 18:7-15
■ Genesis 28:10—29:14;
Matthew 10:27-42

That all this assembly may know that the LORD does not save by sword and spear; for the battle is the LORD's and he will give you into our hand. 1 Samuel 17:47

> "Lord I Lift Your Name on High" (*WoW Worship—Today's 30 Most Powerful Worship Songs* ©1999, Sony/Word)

At my first defense no one came to my support, but all deserted me. May it not be counted against them! But the Lord stood by me and gave me strength, so that through me the message might be fully proclaimed. 2 Timothy 4:16-17

> "You Are My Hiding Place" (*Acoustic Worship 1*, ©1998 BMG/Brentwood)

O Lord, you are our shield from all of our problems. Even if no one else is there for us, we know we can trust in you to always be with us. We feel strength in ourselves through you. Thank you, God. Be our glory, Lord. Amen

WEEK 5

Psalm 18:16-24
Genesis 29:15—30:24;
atthew 11:1-10

was despised and rejected by others; a man of
ffering and acquainted with infirmity. Isaiah 53:3

"Star of the Morning" by Shirley Caesar (*Sailin'*
©1992, Sony/Word)

en Pilate took Jesus and had him flogged.
hn 19:1

"The Hand Song" by Nickel Creek (*Nickel
Creek* ©2000, Sugar Hill)

*heavenly Father, thank you that your Son, Jesus
rist, suffered so much for us. The cruelties done to
m were all to show his love. We truly love Jesus for
he has done for us. Amen*

WEEK 5

wednesday

Psalm 18:25-29
Genesis 30:25—31:21;
atthew 11:11-24

e earth will be full of the knowledge of the LORD as
e waters cover the sea. Isaiah 11:9

"Written on My Heart" by Plus One (*Promise*
©2000, WEA/Atlantic)

od abides in those who confess that Jesus is the Son
God, and they abide in God. So we have known
nd believe the love that God has for us.
John 4:15-16

"King of Glory" by Third Day (*Offering:
Worship Album* ©2000, BMG/Brentwood)

*ear God, Jesus truly is your Son, a King of glory. He
ed so that we could all see your love. We want the
hole world to know how much you are a part of us.
hank you for giving us your love every day. Amen*

WEEK 5

■ Psalm 18:30-36
■ Genesis 31:22-55;
Matthew 11:25—12:8

I have heard your prayer, I have seen your tears.
2 Kings 20:5

"So Help Me God" by dc Talk (*Jesus Freak*
©1995, EMD/Chordant)

And this is the boldness we have in him, that if we
ask anything according to his will, he hears us.
1 John 5:14

"Keep the Candle Burning" by Point of Grace
(*Life Love & Other Mysteries* ©1996,
Sony/Word)

*O sweet Lord, whether we realize it or not, you have
heard our prayers and have seen our tears. Even when
we feel totally alone, you are with us. Please hear our
prayers and help us through both today and tomorrow. Thank you for always being with us. Amen*

WEEK 5

■ Psalm 18:37-45
■ Genesis 32:1-21; Matthew 12:9-21

Give glory to the LORD your God before he brings
darkness. Jeremiah 13:16

"Come, Now Is the Time to Worship" (*WoW
Worship—Today's 30 Most Powerful Worship
Songs* ©1999, Sony/Word)

Your kingdom come. Luke 11:2b

"Change My Heart, Oh God" (*WoW
Worship—Today's 30 Most Powerful Worship
Songs* ©1999, Sony/Word)

*Great God, we always pray "thy kingdom come." We
know that you want the world to be very different
than it is, but we also know that we are part of making that happen. Help us to know how to bring your
light to our world. Help us to understand, forgive,
and most especially, love. Amen*

WEEK 5

Psalm 18:46-50
Genesis 32:22—33:20;
Matthew 12:22-32

ou shall eat your bread to the full, and live securely your land. Leviticus 26:5

"Sweet Glow of Mercy" by Gary Chapman (*Light Inside* ©1994, Reunion)

When they were satisfied, [Jesus] told his disciples, Gather up the fragments left over, so that nothing ay be lost." John 6:12

"Lord, Be Glorified" (*America's 25 Favorite Praise & Worship—Vol. 1* ©1978, BMG/Brentwood)

esus, you teach us so many things, but most of all ou have shown us how endless God's concern is for s. Sometimes we think there is only so much love or orgiveness or food to go around. We're sorry because ou teach us there is no end to how much there is to hare. Amen

WEEK 6

Watchword for the Week
Today, if you hear his voice, do not harden your hearts as in the rebellion. Hebrews 3:15

May] your eyes...be open night and day toward this ouse, the place of which you said, "My name shall be here." 1 Kings 8:29

"I Will Be Here for You" by Michael W. Smith (*WoW 90s—30 Top Christian Songs* ©1999, Sony/Word)

Jesus said,] "Stop making my Father's house a marketlace!" John 2:16

"Sanctuary" (*Acoustic Worship 1* ©1998, BMG/Brentwood Music)

oving God, you have given us families of all kinds. hank you for the way that you nurture us through our ves at home. Help us to see the Spirit working in us nd give us the strength to make our homes your ome. Amen

WEEK 6

■■■ **Psalm 19:1-6**
■■■ **Genesis 34:1-31; Matthew 12:33-45**

Lead me, O LORD, in your righteousness. Psalm 5:8a

> "Guide Me, O Thou Great Jehovah" by John Tesch (*Pure Gospel* ©2001, Faith MD Music)

Guide our feet into the way of peace. Luke 1:79

> "Thy Word" by Amy Grant (*Songs for Worship: Shout to the Lord* ©2001, Time Warner/WEA)

Giver of all life, you are so wonderful in the ways that you have woven the world together. As we read the words you spoke and the words that are written about you, we know that we want to follow you. Help us to go in the direction you want us to and to follow your voice every day. Amen

WEEK 6

■■■ **Psalm 19:7-14**
■■■ **Genesis 35:1—36:8;**
Matthew 12:46—13:2

Yours, O LORD, are the greatness, the power, the glory, the victory, and the majesty; for all that is in the heavens and on the earth is yours. 1 Chronicles 29:11

> "We Bow Down" by Twila Paris (*Almighty God: 17 Timeless Inspirational Performances* ©2001, Provident)

Fear God and give him glory, for the hour of his judgment has come; and worship him who made heaven and earth, the sea and the springs of water. Revelation 14:7

> "Awesome God" by Michael W. Smith (*Awesome God: A Tribute to Rich Mullins* ©1998, Reunion)

Creation. Sky. Water. Land. Hills. Clouds. Trees. Green. White. Snow. Rain. Birds. Insects. Animals. Grain. Humanity. Men. Women. Birth. Babies. Source. Everything. Wisdom. Majesty. Glory. Awesome. Inspiration. Thanks. Amen

WEEK 6

■ Psalm 20
■ Genesis 36:9-43; Matthew 13:3-23

an you find out the deep things of God? Can you
nd out the limit of the Almighty? Job 11:7

"Open Our Eyes" (*WoW Worship—Today's 30
Most Powerful Worship Songs* ©1999,
Sony/Word)

o not claim to be wiser than you are. Romans 12:16

"How Majestic Is Your Name" by Michael W.
Smith (*Songs of Praise* ©1999, Psalm 150
Music)

*ernal God, you are beyond our imaginations. We
y to give you names and describe you, but even all
r words together are not enough for us to know
ou completely or to show your greatness. We're
rry for the times that we limit you, God. You are
uch bigger than that. Amen*

WEEK 6

■ Psalm 21
■ Genesis 37:1-36; Matthew 13:24-43

ok down from heaven and see from your holy and
orious habitation. Where are your zeal and your
ight? Isaiah 63:15a

"He Is Exalted" by Twila Paris (*WoW Worship
Green* ©2001, Sony/Epic)

esus Christ spoke:] "When the Advocate comes,
hom I will send to you from the Father, the Spirit of
uth who comes from the Father, he will testify on
y behalf." John 15:26

"Great Is Thy Faithfulness" by Gary Chapman
(*Shelter* ©1996, Reunion)

*resent Spirit, you work through us to do all the acts
f love and kindness that you want done in our
orld. Open my heart to that Spirit so that I can
now you better and be excited and energized to do
ur work. I always have the power of your Spirit
ith me. Thank you, God. Amen*

WEEK 6

■■■ Psalm 22:1-8
■■■ Genesis 38:1-30; Matthew 13:44-46

The LORD is gracious and merciful, slow to anger, and abounding in steadfast love, and relents from punishing. Joel 2:13

> "The Steadfast Love of the Lord" (*Acoustic Worship 1* ©1998, BMG/Brentwood)

Do you despise the riches of his kindness and forbearance and patience? Do you not realize that God's kindness is meant to lead you to repentance? Romans 2:4

> "What Does the Lord Require!" by Jim Strathdee (*Jubilee* ©1986, Desert Flower Music. See www.strathdeemusic.com)

Kind God, remind us that you are on our side. Forgive us when we live our lives in fear of you or others. There is nothing to fear when we live with you. We pray that your kindness and forgiveness will inspire us to love our friends and family without limits! Amen

WEEK 6

■■■ Psalm 22:9-21
■■■ Genesis 39:1-23; Matthew 13:47-58

Do not trust in these deceptive words: "This is the temple of the LORD, the temple of the LORD."...Truly amend your ways and your doings. Jeremiah 7:4-5

> "They Will Know We Are Christians by Our Love" by Carolyn Arends (*Seize the Day & Other Stories* ©2000, Reunion)

[Jesus Christ spoke:] "When you are offering your gift at the altar, if you remember that your brother or sister has something against you, leave your gift there before the altar and go; first be reconciled to your brother or sister, and then come and offer your gift." Matthew 5:23-24

> "Let the Walls Fall Down" (*Top 25 Kids Praise Songs* ©2000, Maranatha!)

It is amazing, Lord, that you continue to challenge us. Following you means loving the people in our lives in forgiving and renewing ways. If that means swallowing our pride, help us to do that. If that means changing our whole attitude, inspire and lead us. Amen

WEEK 7

sunday

Watchword for the Week
See, we are going up to Jerusalem, and everything that is written about the Son of Man by the prophets will be accomplished. Luke 18:31

..ven though you intended to do harm to me, God ..tended it for good. Genesis 50:20

"Sweet, Sweet Spirit" (*America's 25 Favorite Praise & Worship—Vol. 4* ©1997, Brentwood)

..Ve know that all things work together for good for ..hose who love God, who are called according to his ..urpose. Romans 8:28

"Jehovah" by Amy Grant (*Straight Ahead* ©1984, Myrrh)

..enerous God, everything we have and everything we ..re is because of your kindness to us. There are so ..any gifts that you have given us that we haven't ..ven discovered yet. Give us the wisdom to use our ..fts to honor you. Praise to you, Lord!

WEEK 7

monday

Psalm 22:22-28
Genesis 40:1-23; Matthew 14:1-14

..estore us to yourself, O LORD, that we may be ..estored; renew our days as of old. Lamentations 5:21

"I Surrender All" by Clay Crosse (*I Surrender All* ©1999, Reunion)

..esus spoke to Nicodemus:] "Do not be astonished ..hat I said to you, 'You must be born from above.'" ..ohn 3:7

"Give Me Jesus" by Fernando Ortega (*Home* ©2000, Sony/Word)

..rusted God, you are a wonderful presence in our ..ves. Use all of our lives as raw material to transform ..s into something holy. Help us to see that you ..hange even the most tragic and awful parts of our ..ves into wisdom, strength, and joy. Amen

WEEK 7

■ Psalm 22:29-31
■ Genesis 41:1-57; Matthew 14:15-24

Remember and do not break your covenant with us.
Jeremiah 14:21

> "I Will Delight in the Law of the Lord" by
> Fernando Ortega (*Calvary Chapel Music: Vol.
> 1—Worship Alive* ©1999, Calvary Chapel
> Music)

God has not rejected his people whom he foreknew.
Romans 11:2

> "Our God Reigns" (*America's 25 Favorite Praise
> & Worship—Vol. 1* ©1978, BMG/Brentwood)

*Faithful One, you have never abandoned us and you
never will. We pray that we can see your great love
for us and be inspired to have the same faith so that
we will always turn to you. In Jesus Christ we pray.
Amen.*

WEEK 7

■ Psalm 23
■ Genesis 42:1-38;
Matthew 14:25—15:9

[God] will bless those who fear the LORD, both small
and great. Psalm 115:13

> "I Stand in Awe" (*America's 25 Favorite—Vol.
> 2-Acoustic* ©1999, Brentwood)

Praise our God, all you his servants, and all who fear
him, small and great. Revelation 19:5

> "Shout to the Lord" (*WoW Worship—Today's
> 30 Most Powerful Worship Songs* ©1999,
> Sony/Word)

*Blessed are you, O awesome God! You shower bless-
ings on your people. Help us to live our lives as
blessings to others, witnessing to you with all our
being. Amen*

WEEK 7

■ Psalm 24
Genesis 43:1-34; Matthew 15:10-20

he LORD God is a sun and shield. Psalm 84:11

| "I Am the Light of the World" by Jim Strathdee
(*Light of the World* ©Desert Flower Music. See
www.strathdeemusic.com)

esus spoke:] "I am the light of the world. Whoever
ollows me will never walk in darkness but will have
e light of life." John 8:12

| "Shine, Jesus, Shine" by Graham Kendrick
(*Dove Award Worship* ©2000, Sony/Word)

eading headlines and seeing the TV news is pretty
epressing, O God. Thankfully, we have the good
ews of you and your love to read about also. We
raise you, Friend, because you are our light in the
arkness. Lead us so that we can follow. Amen

WEEK 7

■ Psalm 25:1-7
Genesis 44:1-34; Matthew 15:21-28

ou shall not cheat one another, but you shall fear
our God. Leviticus 25:17

| "Awesome God" by Rich Mullins (*Songs*
©1996, Reunion)

Vhoever loves a brother or sister lives in the light,
nd in such a person there is no cause for stumbling.
John 2:10

| "In the Light" by dc Talk (*Jesus Freak* ©1995,
ForeFront)

wesome Lord and God, forgive us for all the things
e do that do not please you. We hate those things
hen we do them. Help us to be like you and put us
your ever-shining light. Amen

WEEK 7

saturday

▬▬ Psalm 25:8-22
▬▬ Genesis 45:1-28;
Matthew 15:29—16:4

O God, do not forsake me, until I proclaim your might to all the generations to come. Psalm 71:18

> "For Future Generations" by 4Him (*The Ride* ©1994, BMG/Verity Music)

My grace is sufficient for you, for my power is made perfect in weakness. 2 Corinthians 12:9

> "Get Down" by Audio Adrenaline (*Underdog* ©1999, Sparrow)

Lord of all generations, you have taught us how to become humble through your Son. Thank you for lifting us up when we become humble for you. Keep us strong in faith so we can proclaim your Word to everyone. Amen

WEEK 8

sunday

Watchword for the Week
The Son of God was revealed for this purpose, to destroy the works of the devil. 1 John 3:8

He made intercession for the transgressors. Isaiah 53:12

> "Free" by Ginny Owens (*Without Condition* ©1999, Sony/Word)

[Jesus spoke:] "Love your enemies and pray for those who persecute you, so that you may be children of your Father in heaven." Matthew 5:44-45

> "I Want to Be Just Like You" by Phillips, Craig, & Dean (*Lifeline* ©1994, Star Song)

Freeing Lord, thank you for unlocking the chains of sin that held us down. We are free because of your sacrifice. Help us to show you to others by being an example of your love and being like you, our Father. Amen

■ Psalm 26
■ Genesis 46:1-24; Matthew 16:5-20

■ LORD, be gracious to us; we wait for you.
aiah 33:2

> "Draw Me Close" by the Katinas (*Exodus* ©1998, Rocketown)

esus spoke to his disciples:] "You will weep and ourn, but your pain will turn into joy." John 16:20

> "Four Days Late" by Karen Peck & New River (*A Taste of Grace* ©Spring Hill)

ll-knowing Lord, thank you for your wisdom. You now when the time is right. You do things for the od of your glory even if we cannot see it. Help us be open to your timing and actions. Amen

■ Psalm 27:1-6
■ Genesis 46:25—47:31; Matthew 16:21-28

ut Balaam replied, "Although Balak were to give me s house full of silver and gold, I could not go eyond the command of the LORD my God." umbers 22:18

> "I Will Follow Christ" by Clay Crosse (*I Surrender All* ©1999, BMG/Verity)

Paul wrote:] "Am I now seeking human approval, or od's approval? Or am I trying to please people? If I ere still pleasing people, I would not be a servant of hrist." Galatians 1:10

> "In Not Of" by Avalon (*In a Different Light* ©1999, EMD/Sparrow)

uler of everything, guide us into the world with your ve. Guide us and help us spread your word to the orld without falling into its hands. Keep us close to ou and your love and we will wear your name with o fear. Amen

WEEK 8

■ Psalm 27:7-14
■ Genesis 48:1-22; Matthew 17:1-13

See now, I am for you; I will turn to you, and you shall be tilled and sown. Ezekiel 36:9

> "Written on My Heart" by Plus One (*The Promise* ©2000, Chordant)

[Mary said:] "He has helped his servant Israel, in remembrance of his mercy, according to the promise he made to our ancestors, to Abraham and to his descendants forever." Luke 1:54-55

> "I Am the Way" by Mark Schultz (*Mark Schultz* ©2000, Sony/Word)

Always-present Guide, we don't know where we would be without you. Thank you for always being with us even when we didn't know it. Thank you for your love and for being the answer to all of life's problems. Amen

WEEK 8

■ Psalm 28
■ Genesis 49:1-33; Matthew 17:14-27

Thus says the LORD: In a time of favor I have answered you, on a day of salvation I have helped you. Isaiah 49:8

> "Stranded" by Plumb (*candycoatedwaterdrops* ©1999, Brentwood)

At an acceptable time I have listened to you, and [in the] day of salvation I have helped you. 2 Corinthians 6:2

> "Away from You" by the O.C. Supertones (*Chase the Sun* ©1999, EMD/BEC)

Forever Helper, there is nothing in this world that doesn't contain you. Thank you for always being around to help us. As we go through this day, help us to follow your way even if it looks hard and we're afraid. Amen

WEEK 8

friday

■ Psalm 29
■ Genesis 50:1-26; Matthew 18:1-14

They rise in the darkness as a light for the upright;
they are gracious, merciful, and righteous.
Psalm 112:4

> "Reborn" by Rebecca St. James (*Transform*
> ©2000, Chordant)

The darkness is passing away and the true light is
already shining. Whoever says, "I am in the light,
while hating a brother or sister, is still in the darkness." 1 John 2:8-9

> "Gather at the River" by Point of Grace (*The
> Whole Truth* ©1995, Sony/Word)

Lord, you are an example to us all. Sometimes we
don't agree with others and we get angry with each
other. Help us to get together with those persons so
we can enjoy forgiveness from each other. If we are
to be reborn in Christ, we must change to be more
like you. Amen

WEEK 8

saturday

■ Psalm 30:1-5
■ Exodus 1:1—2:10; Matthew 18:15-35

Truly God is good to the upright, to those who are
pure in heart. Psalm 73:1

> "Alabaster Box" by CeCe Winans (*Alabaster
> Box* ©1999, Chordant)

"Blessed are the pure in heart, for they will see God."
Matthew 5:8

> "I Want to Know You (In the Secret)" by
> Sonicflood (*Sonicpraise* ©2000, Chordant)

God of wonder, you are the only one who can truly
judge us. Only you know where each heart is. Help
us to give everything to you so that we can be open
and pure. For we want to know you like you know
us. Amen

WEEK 9

Watchword for the Week
God proves his love for us in that while we still were sinners Christ died for us. Romans 5:8

Go now, see if it is well with your brothers. Genesis 37:14

"More Than You'll Ever Know" by Watermark (*All Things New* ©2000, Rocketown)

My friends, if anyone is detected in a transgression, you who have received the Spirit should restore such a one in a spirit of gentleness. Galatians 6:1

"Hands and Feet" by Audio Adrenaline (*Underdog* ©1999, EMI/Chordant)

Father of us all, help us to become like you so we can guide our brothers and sisters to you. We want to help as many people as we can to find you. Thank you for the people in our lives who helped us to find you and your love. Amen

WEEK 9

▨▨ Psalm 30:6-12
▨▨ Exodus 2:11—3:22; Matthew 19:1-12

He will again have compassion upon us; he will tread our iniquities under foot. You will cast all our sins into the depths of the sea. Micah 7:19

"Always Have, Always Will" by Avalon (*In a Different Light* ©1999, EMD/Sparrow)

[Jesus Christ] is the atoning sacrifice for our sins, and not for ours only but also for the sins of the whole world. 1 John 2:2

"Into You" by Jennifer Knapp (*Lay It Down* ©2000, EMD/Chordant)

Compassionate God, thank you for being gentle with us. We are all sinners and fall short every day. You are an incredible God for your forgiveness over and over again. We will try to be sinless because we love you. Thank you for always loving and forgiving us. Amen

WEEK 9

Psalm 31:1-5
Exodus 4:1—5:10; Matthew 19:13-26

[Th]ere is no perversion of justice with the LORD our [G]od. 2 Chronicles 19:7

"Alleluia/I Love You Lord" by Go Fish (*Go Fish Live: Created for This* ©2000, inpop/Chordant)

[M]y brothers and sisters, as believers in our glorious [Lo]rd Jesus Christ, don't show favoritism. James 2:1 [N]IV)

"Show You Love" by Jaci Velasquez (*Jaci Velasquez* ©1998, Sony/Word)

[Fa]ther God, you created us all and love us all. Help [us] to love everyone as you do. You have shown each [an]d every one of us grace. Help us to do the same. [Bu]t also help us to not weaken our faith in so doing. [A]men

WEEK 9

Psalm 31:6-9
Exodus 5:11—6:12;
[M]atthew 19:27-30

[W]hen the poor and needy seek water, and there is [n]one, and their tongue is parched with thirst, I the [LO]RD will answer them. Isaiah 41:17

"The Only Thing I Need" by 4Him with Jon Anderson of Yes (*Streams* ©1999, Sony/Word)

[J]esus spoke to the Samaritan woman:] "Everyone [w]ho drinks of this water will be thirsty again, but [th]ose who drink of the water that I will give them will [n]ever be thirsty. The water that I will give will become [in] them a spring of water gushing up to eternal life." [Jo]hn 4:13-14

"Revive Us" by Anointed (*Anointed* ©1999, Sony/Word)

[A]lways-present Redeemer, thank you for being with [u]s always. All that we need we already have in you. [H]elp us to constantly thirst for you, Lord. Amen

WEEK 9

■■ Psalm 31:10-20
■■ Exodus 6:13—7:24; Matthew 20:1-16

You, our God, have punished us less than our iniquities deserved. Ezra 9:13

> "Sanctuary" by Chris Rodriguez (*Streams* ©1999, Sony/Word)

For our sake he made him to be sin who knew no sin, so that in him we might become the righteousness of God. 2 Corinthians 5:21

> "Where I Wanna Be" by V*Enna (*Where I Wanna Be* ©2000, Essential Records)

Living Sanctuary, we often seem to always find ourselves away from you. Yet you still cover us with your love and protection. We want to be in the center of your plan. We want to be like the one who died for our sins. Help us to do this every day. Amen

WEEK 9

■■ Psalm 31:21-24
■■ Exodus 8:1-32; Matthew 20:17-28

Turn to me and be gracious to me, for I am lonely and afflicted. Psalm 25:16

> "My Only Hope Is in You" by Truth (*Never Be the Same* ©1998, Pamplin)

The sick man answered [Jesus], "Sir, I have no one to put me into the pool when the water is stirred up; and while I am making my way, someone else steps down ahead of me." Jesus said to him, "Stand up, take your mat and walk." John 5:7-8

> "The Gentle Healer" by Michael Card (*The Life* ©1988. For more information, click on www.michaelcard.com)

Lord, we praise you today for taking care of us—for comforting us when we are lonely, for healing us when no one else even knows we are hurting. Continue to bless us, keep us safe, and love us. Amen

■ Psalm 32
Exodus 9:1-35;
atthew 20:29—21:11

is] said, "It is vain to serve God. What do we profit
keeping his command or by going about as
urners before the LORD of hosts?..." The LORD
ok note and listened. Malachi 3:14, 16

 "We Can Make a Difference" by Jaci Velasquez
(*Heavenly Place* ©1996, Sony/Word)

aul wrote:] "Think of us in this way: as servants of
rist and stewards of God's mysteries."
Corinthians 4:1

"Live the Life" by Michael W. Smith (*Live the Life* ©1998, Reunion)

ving Savior, you have given us the greatest exam-
e of serving God with our whole beings. Help us to
'low you in praising God, sacrificing of ourselves,
d being good stewards of all that God has given us.
men

Watchword for the Week

No one who puts a hand to the
plow and looks back is fit for the
kingdom of God. Luke 9:62

Ephraim my dear son? Is he the child I delight in? As
ten as I speak against him, I still remember him.
erefore I am deeply moved for him; I will surely have
ercy on him, says the LORD. Jeremiah 31:20

"With Arms Wide Open" by Creed (*Human Clay* ©1999, Wind-Up)

od, who is rich in mercy, out of the great love with
hich he loved us even when we were dead through
ur trespasses, made us alive together with Christ.
hesians 2:4-5

"Love Song for a Savior" by Jars of Clay (*Jars of Clay* ©1995, BMG/Jive/Silvertone)

oly God, there is nothing we can do to stop your
ercy that washes over us endlessly. When we sin,
u forgive us. When we forsake you, you still love us.
ank you for loving us as your children. Amen

WEEK 10

monday

■ Psalm 33:1-5
■ Exodus 10:1-29; Matthew 21:12-22

Keep your voice from weeping, and your eyes from tears; for there is a reward for your work, says the LORD. Jeremiah 31:16

"Keep Your Head Up" Excelsior (*God at Work* ©2001, Verity)

[Jesus Christ said:] "Blessed are you who weep now, for you will laugh." Luke 6:21

"You Don't Have to Be Afraid" by Take 6 (*Brothers* ©1996, WEA/Warner Brothers)

Sometimes it seems that there is no hope. Sometimes it seems like it would be easier to give up on life and love. But, Lord, you are always there. You promise us the things that the world cannot give. Our hope is always in you, Lord, because you are our reward. Amen

WEEK 10

tuesday

■ Psalm 33:6-11
■ Exodus 11:1—12:30; Matthew 21:23-32

I will delight in my people; no more shall the sound of weeping be heard in it, or the cry of distress. Isaiah 65:19

"You Will Never Walk Alone" by Point of Grace (*Free to Fly* ©2001, Word)

We wait for new heavens and a new earth, where righteousness is at home. 2 Peter 3:13

"Darkness into Light" by Paige (*Paige* ©2001, Word)

Loving Parent, you wipe away all our tears and hold us in your arms. Even when we are afraid, you promise to be with us. You offer us a home with you forever, where righteousness and peace will surround us. Let us always look to you for everything we need. Amen

wednesday

Psalm 33:12-22
Exodus 12:31-51; Matthew 21:33-46

Your sun shall no more go down, or your moon withdraw itself; for the LORD will be your everlasting light. Isaiah 60:20

"Father of Lights" by John Barnet (*I Love Your Presence* ©2001, EMD/Chordant)

God is light and in him there is no darkness at all…If we walk in the light as he himself is in the light, we have fellowship with one another, and the blood of Jesus his Son cleanses us from all sin. 1 John 1:5, 7

"Go Light Your World" by Kathy Troccoli (*Sounds of Heaven* ©1995, Reunion)

Eternal Light, you were given to us to show us the way. You illumine our paths and guide us no matter where we are. We are grateful that we never need to fear darkness. Help us to spread your light in our world, so that everyone can know the hope that we know. Amen

thursday

Psalm 34:1-7
**Exodus 13:1—14:18;
Matthew 22:1-14**

You came near when I called on you; you said, "Do not fear!" Lamentations 3:57

"Arms of Love" by Amy Grant (*Age to Age* ©1982, Myrrh)

[The disciples] urged [Jesus] strongly, saying, "Stay with us, because it is almost evening and the day is now nearly over." So he went in to stay with them. Luke 24:29

"Hold Me Jesus" by Rich Mullins (*Songs* ©1996, Reunion)

Jesus, you answer every prayer we have, including the prayer to stay with us forever. We know you are near, and we will not be afraid. Hold us when we need to feel your presence even more strongly. Amen

WEEK 10

■■■ **Psalm 34:8-18**
■■■ **Exodus 14:19—15:18;**
Matthew 22:15-22

The man and his wife hid themselves from the presence of the LORD God. Genesis 3:8b

> "Go and Sin No More" by Rebecca St. James (*God* ©1996, EMD/Chordant)

For all who do evil hate the light and do not come to the light, so that their deeds may not be exposed. But those who do what is true come to the light, so that it may be clearly seen that their deeds have been done in God. John 3:20-21

> "Bearers of the Light" by Michael Card (*Poiema* ©1994, EMD/Sparrow)

Mighty God, we are in awe of your presence. At times we are ashamed of ourselves and our actions. In the power of your light, we feel unworthy. Help us to come to you for forgiveness so that we need not be ashamed. You will be merciful. Let us strive to be lights in our world and live the way you want us to live. Amen

WEEK 10

■■■ **Psalm 34:19-22**
■■■ **Exodus 15:19—16:36;**
Matthew 22:23-40

How very good and pleasant it is when kindred live together in unity! Psalm 133:1

> "Love One Another" by Kathy Troccoli (*Love and Mercy* ©1997, Reunion)

As you, Father, are in me and I am in you, may they also be in us, so that the world may believe that you have sent me. John 17:21

> "This Must Be the Lamb" by Michael Card (*Signature Songs* ©1999. For more information, click on www.michaelcard.com)

O Lord, the gift you gave us in the person of Jesus is beyond our comprehension. We do not deserve this kind of love and in many ways we do not even know how to accept it. Mold us into the people you would have us be, that we may be united and live peaceably with other believers. Amen

sunday

Watchword for the Week

Unless a grain of wheat falls into the earth and dies, it remains just a single grain; but if it dies, it bears much fruit. John 12:24

[If] you, O LORD, should mark iniquities, LORD, who could stand? Psalm 130:3

"Sweet Glow of Mercy" by Gary Chapman (*Light Inside* ©1994, Reunion)

[Jesus Christ spoke:] "Anyone who hears my word and believes him who sent me has eternal life, and does not come under judgment, but has passed from death to life." John 5:24

"As It Is in Heaven" by Michael W. Smith (*I'll Lead You Home* ©1995, Reunion)

How amazing is the mercy you have for us, Lord! You have given us a Savior that washes away our sins. Not only do you forgive us, but you do not even remember our sins. Without your grace, we could not even exist. With your grace, we will live with you forever. Amen

monday

Psalm 35:1-10
Exodus 17:1—18:6;
Matthew 22:41—23:7

[I] am the LORD, I have called you in righteousness, I have taken you by the hand and kept you; I have given you as a covenant to the people, a light to the nations, to open the eyes that are blind, to bring out the prisoners from the dungeon, from the prison those who sit in darkness. Isaiah 42:6-7

"Commit Your Life" by John Michael Talbot (*Simple Heart* ©2000, EMD/Chordant)

[The] eyes of all in the synagogue were fixed on [Jesus]. Then he began to say to them, "Today this scripture has been fulfilled in your hearing." Luke 4:20-21

"The Book" by Michael Card (*Songs from the Book* ©1999, Sony/Word)

Dear God, your Scriptures are a precious gift to us. Through them we learn about you and your love for all your people. Help us to commit our lives to you, as we know you through your word. You have made our mission clear. Help us to accept it so that we can be a light to the nations. Amen

WEEK 11

■ Psalm 35:11-18
■ Exodus 18:7—19:9; Matthew 23:8-22

Can mortals make for themselves gods? Such are no gods! Jerèmiah 16:20

| "We Shall Behold Him" by Sandi Patti (*Finest Moments* ©1990, Sony/Word)

Keep yourselves from idols. 1 John 5:21

| "Bound to Come Some Trouble" by Rich Mullins (*Never Picture Perfect* ©1989, Reunion)

Source of all life, you are all we need. You have created us, and everything around us. Yet we often look to other places and people for things we only think we need. Lord, remove the distractions and help us focus on you. Then we will find all we really need is what we have already been given. Amen

WEEK 11

■ Psalm 35:19-28
■ Exodus 19:10—20:21; Matthew 23:23-32

God has made me fruitful in the land of my misfortunes. Genesis 41:52

| "My Hope Is You" by Third Day (*Offerings* ©1997, BMG/Brentwood)

Even though our outer nature is wasting away, our inner nature is being renewed day by day. 2 Corinthians 4:16

| "Living Water" by Bob Carlisle (*Butterfly Kisses* ©1997, BMG/Verity)

Creator, our bodies and everything in this world will fade away. We have encountered hard times and great pain. But these are not the things that will last. We praise you for constantly renewing and refreshing our spirits and giving us opportunities to love and serve you. Amen

WEEK 11

thursday

- Psalm 36
- Exodus 20:22—21:27;
  Matthew 23:33-39

e precepts of the LORD are right, rejoicing the heart.
alm 19:8a

"Whose Report Shall You Believe" by Ron
Kenoly (*Lift Him Up* ©1997, Sony/Word)

this we may be sure that we know him, if we obey
commandments. 1 John 2:3

"Higher Ways" by Steven Curtis Chapman (*For
the Sake of the Call* ©1990, EMD/Sparrow)

od, you have shown us what is right and good. We
n trust you and your leading. You have been faith-
to us; make us faithful to you. Lead us so that we
ll obey you, and love us when we fall short. As we
ive to do your will, make us a blessing to others.
men

WEEK 11

friday

- Psalm 37:1-6
- Exodus 21:28—22:24;
  Matthew 24:1-25

o not remember the former things, or consider the
ings of old. I am about to do a new thing; now it
rings forth, do you not perceive it? Isaiah 43:18-19

"Lord I Believe in You" by Crystal Lewis (*Gold*
©1998, UNI/Gospocentric)

e kingdom of God is like a mustard seed that some-
e took and sowed in the garden; it grew and
ecame a tree. Luke 13:19

"'Akehlulek' Ubaba (With God Everything Is
Possible)" by Ladysmith Black Mambazo and
Charlie Peacock (*Roaring Lambs* ©2000, Squint)

od of wonderful surprises, you work beyond our
ildest imaginations. Thank you for making us a part
your amazing plan. Never let our human doubt or
ar stand in the way of your power. Bring us to
ceptance and love of your mystery. Amen

WEEK 11

■ Psalm 37:7-15
■ Exodus 22:25—23:26;
Matthew 24:26-35

Let the wicked forsake their way, and the unrighteous their thoughts; let them return to the LORD, that he may have mercy on them. Isaiah 55:7

> "Much Afraid" by Jars of Clay (*Much Afraid* ©1997, BMG/Jive/Silvertone)

[Paul wrote:] "For I am the least of the apostles, unfit to be called an apostle, because I persecuted the church of God. But by the grace of God I am what I am…." 1 Corinthians 15:9-10

> "Love's Been Following You" Twila Paris (*Where I Stand* ©1996, EMD/Sparrow)

Lord Jesus, we bow before you today recognizing our unworthiness. Yet you love us anyway. We can never repay you for that kind of love. Accept our apologies and sincerest confessions so that nothing can interfere with your amazing love. Amen

WEEK 12

Watchword for the Week
The Son of Man came not to be served but to serve, and to give his life a ransom for many.
Matthew 20:28

This is God, our God forever and ever. He will be our guide forever. Psalm 48:14

> "I Will Be Here" by Steven Curtis Chapman (*Greatest Hits* ©1997, Sparrow)

Then Peter came to himself and said, "Now I am sure that the Lord has sent his angel and rescued me from the hands of Herod." Acts 12:11

> "Irish Sea" by Margaret Becker (*Falling Forward* ©1998, Sparrow)

Our trust and confidence is in you, Lord. Lead us and guide us by the power of your mighty hand. Empower us to greet the challenges of this day knowing that you are present and active in our lives. Amen

WEEK 12

Psalm 37:16-22
Exodus 23:27—25:9;
Matthew 24:36-44

ou shall not be partial to the poor or defer to the
eat: with justice you shall judge your neighbor.
viticus 19:15

"Deeper" by Delirious? (*King of Fools*
©EMD/Sparrow)

ve as children of light—for the fruit of the light is
und in all that is good and right and true.
ohesians 5:8-9

"I Have Decided" by Michael Card (*Signature
Songs* ©1999, Benson)

ord, help us to do your will today. *Inspire us to
ach out to the poor, the blind, the naked, the sick.
se us as instruments of your grace and mercy. Amen*

WEEK 12

Psalm 37:23-26
Exodus 25:10-40; Matthew 24:45-51

ou shall not revile the deaf or put a stumbling block
efore the blind; you shall fear your God.
eviticus 19:14

"I, the Lord of Sea and Sky (Here I Am, Lord)"
by the Wells Cathedral Choir (*English Hymn 1*
©1999)

Vhen you give a banquet, invite the poor, the crip-
led, the lame, and the blind. And you will be blessed,
ecause they cannot repay you. Luke 14:13-14

"We Can Make a Difference" by Jaci Velasquez
(*A Heavenly Place* ©1996, Myrrh)

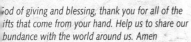

od of giving and blessing, thank you for all of the
ifts that come from your hand. *Help us to share our
bundance with the world around us. Amen*

WEEK 12

Psalm 37:27-33
Exodus 26:1-37; Matthew 25:1-13

O LORD, for your name's sake; our apostasies indeed are many, and we have sinned against you. Jeremiah 14:7

"Undo Me" by Jennifer Knapp (*Kansas* ©1998, Gotee)

Our hearts condemn us; [but] God is greater than our hearts, and he knows everything. 1 John 3:20

"Between You and Me" by dc Talk (*Jesus Freak* ©1995, EMD/Chordant)

Lord Jesus, lift the burdens from our hearts. Our transgressions are, indeed, many, but you and you alone have the power to forgive us, to cancel our debt, to make us whole again. Amen

WEEK 12

Psalm 37:34-40
Exodus 27:1—28:14;
Matthew 25:14-30

The LORD is a refuge for his people, a stronghold for the people of Israel. Joel 3:16

"Walk on Water" by Audio Adrenaline (*Bloom* ©1996, ForeFront)

If God is for us, who is against us? Romans 8:31

"Anything" by PFR (*Them* ©1996, Sparrow)

Lord, help us do something radical for you this day. Encourage our steps of faith as we share your love and preach your gospel. Amen

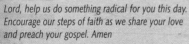

friday

Psalm 38:1-8
Exodus 28:15-43; Matthew 25:31-46

merciful to me, O God, be merciful to me, for in
my soul takes refuge. Psalm 57:1

"Body and Soul" by Susan Ashton (*A Distant
Call* ©1996, Sparrow)

m his fullness we have all received, grace upon
ce. John 1:16

"No One Loves Me Like You" by Jars of Clay (*If
I Left the Zoo* ©1999, BMG/Jive/Silvertone)

d of graciousness, teach us that you and your
rcy are enough for us in this world, and in the
rld to come. Amen

---

saturday

Psalm 38:9-16
Exodus 29:1-32; Matthew 26:1-13

heals the brokenhearted, and binds up their
unds. Psalm 147:3

"Awesome in the Place" Dave Billington
(*Acoustic Worship, Volume 2* ©1999,
BMG/Brentwood)

zarus was ill. So [his] sisters sent a message to
us, "Lord, he whom you love is ill." John 11:2-3

"Get Down" by Audio Adrenaline (*Underdog*
©1999, ForeFront)

ng healing and wholeness to our bodies, minds,
d spirits. Make us complete and perfect in your
ns. We offer ourselves to you for service, ministry,
d witness. Amen

WEEK 13

Watchword for the Week
The Son of Man must be lifted up, that whoever believes in him may have eternal life. John 3:14-15

Thus says the LORD of hosts: Return to me, says the LORD of hosts, and I will return to you. Zechariah 1:3

"God So Loved" by Jaci Velasquez (*Jaci Velasquez* ©1998, Myrrh)

The great crowd that had come to the festival heard that Jesus was coming to Jerusalem. So they took branches of palm trees and went out to meet him, shouting, "Hosanna! Blessed is the one who comes in the name of the Lord—the King of Israel!" John 12:12-13

"Agnus Dei" by Third Day (*Exodus* ©1998, Sony/Word)

Today we join the crowd praising you and welcoming you as king of our hearts and our souls. We offer up to you our prayers of thanksgiving for your power and reign. Amen

---

WEEK 13

■ Psalm 38:17-22
■ Exodus 29:33—30:16; Matthew 26:14-30

LORD, do not let the downtrodden be put to shame.... Psalm 74:21

"You Are My All in All" by Dennis Jernigan (*You Are My All in All* ©2000, Here to Him)

Then Jesus said to [Zacchaeus], "Today salvation has come to this house." Luke 19:9

"I'm Found in You" by Stephen Curtis Chapman (*Greatest Hits* ©1997, Sparrow Records)

Redeemer and preserver of life, your power and ability to find us when we are lost and restore us when we have fallen apart is truly remarkable. Where would we be without you? Amen

tuesday

Psalm 39:1-6
Exodus 30:17—31:11;
Matthew 26:31-35

sweep them away; they are like a dream, like
...s that is renewed in the morning; in the morning
...ourishes and is renewed; in the evening it fades
...withers. Psalm 90:5-6

"Amazing" by Point of Grace (*Steady On*
©1998, Sony/Word)

...at which] is sown in weakness is raised in power.
...orinthians 15:43

"Never Been Unloved" by Michael W. Smith
(*Live the Life* ©1998, Reunion)

*...d, you have set us free from the power of sin and
...th, yet we cling to the very things that are sinful
...deadly. Help us to cling to you and your great
...er to make all things new. Amen*

wednesday

Psalm 39:7-13
Exodus 31:12—32:29;
Matthew 26:36-46

...med you, you are my servant; O Israel, you will
...be forgotten by me. Isaiah 44:21

"Someday" by Michael W. Smith (*I'll Lead You
Home* ©1995, Reunion)

...God rejected his people? By no means!
...mans 11:1

"Healing Waters" by Michael Tumes (*WoW
1999* ©1996, EMD/Chordant)

*...d of faithfulness, from the very beginning of
...ation you have been steadfast in your love for us.
...ay, we take confidence in your promise to be with
...always. Amen*

WEEK 13

■ Psalm 40:1-8
■ Exodus 32:30—33:23;
Matthew 26:47-58

Thus says the LORD: "Do not let the wise boast in their wisdom, do not let the mighty boast in their might, do not let the wealthy boast in their wealth." Jeremiah 9:23

> "As It Is in Heaven" by Michael W. Smith (*I'll Lead You Home* ©1995, Reunion)

Whoever does not love does not know God, for God is love. 1 John 4:8

> "That's How Much I Love You" by Kathy Troccoli (*Sounds of Heaven* ©1995, Reunion)

God, your love turns things upside down and inside out—bringing the wise and wealthy down and uplifting the poor and lowly. May we be so immersed in your love that we are brought low daily and rise to live in your behalf. Amen

---

WEEK 13

■ Psalm 40:9-17
■ Exodus 34:1-35; Matthew 26:59-75

Who provides for the raven its prey, when its young ones cry to God, and wander about for lack of food? Job 38:41

> "Hope to Carry On" by Rich Mullins (*Songs 2* ©1999, Reunion)

[Jesus Christ said:] "I am the bread of life." John 6:48

> "Saving the World" by Clay Crosse (*Stained Glass* ©1997, Reunion)

Lord of life, help us to heed your call to unity. With your body and blood you molded us together. Use us to reveal your continued love and faithfulness to all the people and the world around us. Amen

saturday

Psalm 41
Exodus 35:1-35; Matthew 27:1-10

ive thanks to you, O God; we give thanks; your
is near. People tell of your wondrous deeds.
75:1

"Shout to the Lord" by Darlene Zschech (*Dove
Award Worship* ©2000, Sony/Word)

depth of the riches and wisdom and knowledge
od! How unsearchable are his judgments and
inscrutable his ways! Romans 11:33

"Steady On" by Point of Grace (*Steady On*
©1998, Sony/Word)

*praise you, mysterious God! Your ways are not
vays, but when we look at the wonder of our
we cannot help but proclaim your wondrous
s. Help us to honor you with our lives. Amen*

sunday

Watchword for the Week
[Christ said:] "I was dead, and see, I
am alive forever and ever; and I
have the keys of Death and of
Hades." Revelation 1:18

ouse lies in ruins, while all of you hurry off to
own houses. Therefore the heavens above you
withheld the dew, and the earth has withheld its
uce. Haggai 1:9-10

"Be Thou My Vision" by Michael Card
(*Starkinder-Celtic Conversation* ©1998,
Sony/Word)

st] died for all, so that those who live might live
onger for themselves, but for him who died and
raised for them. 2 Corinthians 5:15

"Worlds Apart" by Jars of Clay (*Jars of Clay*
©1995, Brentwood)

*, Jesus Christ, open the tombs of our lives that we
t know the true power of your resurrection. Help
share your great news of everlasting life and
ation. Amen*

WEEK 14

■ Psalm 42
■ Exodus 36:1-38; Matthew 27:11-31

How great are [God's] signs, how mighty his wonders!
His kingdom is an everlasting kingdom, and his
sovereignty is from generation to generation.
Daniel 4:3

> "Ancient of Days" by Insyderz (*Skalleluia!*
> ©1998, Squint)

God put this power to work in Christ when he raised
him from the dead and seated him at his right hand in
the heavenly places, far above all rule and authority
and power and dominion, and above every name that
is named, not only in this age but also in the age to
come. Ephesians 1:20-21

> "God of Wonders" by Mac Powell and Cliff
> Danielle Young (*City on a Hill* ©2000,
> BMG/Jive/Silvertone)

*Lord, we are thankful to call you that. You are worthy
of all our praise and adoration. We pray now and
always for your will to reign supreme in our hearts.
Amen*

WEEK 14

■ Psalm 43
■ Exodus 37:1-29; Matthew 27:32-44

It is good that one should wait quietly for the salvation of the LORD. Lamentations 3:26

> "Deep Enough to Dream" by Chris Rice (*Deep
> Enough to Dream* ©1997 Sony/Word)

God will wipe away every tear from their eyes.
Revelation 7:17b

> "Trading My Sorrows" by Max Lucado (*When
> Christ Comes* ©1999, Sony/Word)

*Today, Lord, we ask you to fill our hearts with the
power of your spirit. Lead us to a quiet place where
we can learn more about ourselves and you. Amen*

WEEK 14

wednesday

Psalm 44:1-8
Exodus 38:1-31; Matthew 27:45-56

You shall not steal; you shall not deal falsely; and you shall not lie to one another. Leviticus 19:11

"My Will" by dc Talk (*Intermission: Greatest Hits* ©2000, EMD/Chordant)

[Do no] wrong nor exploit a brother or sister, because the Lord is an avenger in all these things.
Thessalonians 4:6

"This World" by Caedmon's Call (*Caedmon's Call* ©1997 WEA/Warner)

O God, we confess to you our many sins that separate us from you and ask for forgiveness. Help us to stand up against this world that is full of sin, and trust in your reign over it. Amen

WEEK 14

thursday

Psalm 44:9-16
Exodus 39:1-31; Matthew 27:57-66

Be glad and rejoice in the Lord your God. Joel 2:23

"Let Everything That Has Breath" by Passion Worship Band (*Passion: Better Is One Day* ©2000 EMD/Sparrow)

Rejoice in the Lord always; again I will say, rejoice. Let your gentleness be known to everyone. The Lord is near. Philippians 4:4-5

"Gloria" by Small Town Poets (*Listen Closely* ©1998 EMD/Chordant)

Lord, let us not forget where our true joy comes from. In everything life throws our way today help us to be happy that we are your children. Amen

WEEK 14

■ Psalm 44:17-26
■ Exodus 39:32—40:23;
Matthew 28:1-15

Be very careful, therefore, to love the LORD your God.
Joshua 23:11

> "My Hope Is You" by Third Day (*Conspiracy #5*
> ©1997, BMG/Jive/Silvertone)

Let us take care that none of you should seem to
have failed to reach [the promise of entering his rest].
Hebrews 4:1

> "Testify to Love" by Avalon (*Maze of Grace*
> ©1997, EMD/Chordant)

Thank you, Lord, for showing us what love is through
the example of your Son Jesus. We pray that we
share that love every day with those around us and
with you, our king. Amen

WEEK 14

■ Psalm 45:1-9
■ Exodus 40:24; Leviticus 1:17;
Matthew 28:16; Mark 1:8

Be exalted, O God, above the heavens. Let your glory
be over all the earth. Psalm 57:5

> "Hallelujahs" by Chris Rice (*Deep Enough to*
> *Dream* ©1997, Sony/Word)

Hallelujah! For the Lord our God the Almighty reigns.
Let us rejoice and exult and give him the glory.
Revelation 19:6-7

> "Be Glorified" by Passion Worship Band
> (*Passion: Better Is One Day* ©2000,
> EMD/Sparrow)

Father almighty we praise your name. This world is
full of many wonders and we join with them in
professing how great you are. Amen

sunday

Watchword for the Week

Blessed be the God and Father of our Lord Jesus Christ! By his great mercy he has given us a new birth into a living hope through the resurrection of Jesus Christ from the dead. 1 Peter 1:3

...sh me thoroughly from my iniquity, and cleanse me ...m my sin. Psalm 51:2

"His Grace Is Sufficient" by Jennifer Knapp (*Kansas* ©1998, Chordant)

...ve confess our sins, he who is faithful and just will ...give us our sins and cleanse us from all unrighteous... ...s. 1 John 1:9

"Hold It Up to the Light" by Small Town Poets (*Listen Closely* ©1998, EMD/Chordant)

...d, thank you for the assurance of a new beginning ...en we ask you for forgiveness. May we always be ...ck to admit when we fall short of your glory and ...ays be steady in your grace. Amen

monday

Psalm 45:10-17
Leviticus 2:1—3:17; Mark 1:9-20

...awesome deeds you answer us with deliverance, O ...d of our salvation; you are the hope of all the ends ...the earth and of the farthest seas. Psalm 65:5

"I Could Sing of Your Love Forever" by Sonicflood (*Sonicflood* ©1999, EMD/Chordant)

...us Christ came and proclaimed peace to you who ...re far off and peace to those who were near. ...esians 2:17

"Shout to the North" by Delirious? (*Cutting Edge* ©1997 EMD/Sparrow)

...d, you reign over all creation and grant us peace ...erever we are in life. Help us to share your won- ...s with everyone we are around. Amen

WEEK 15

■ Psalm 46
■ Leviticus 4:1-35; Mark 1:21-34

With my God I can leap over a wall. Psalm 18:29

> "Free" by Steven Curtis Chapman (*Signs of Life* ©1996, EMD/Sparrow)

[Christ] is our peace; in his flesh he has made both groups into one and has broken down the dividing wall, that is, the hostility between us. Ephesians 2:14

> "Stand" by Bebo Norman (*Ten Thousand Days* ©1999, BMG/Brentwood)

Dear Lord, may we unite with fellow believers as one in the Spirit. We pray that your love will bring us together. May we stand together as your people, devoted and ready to change the world in which we live. Amen

WEEK 15

■ Psalm 47
■ Leviticus 5:1—6:13; Mark 1:35-45

You, God, forgave and were gracious and merciful, slow to anger and abounding in steadfast love. Nehemiah 9:17

> "Mansions" by Burlap to Cashmere (*Anybody Out There?* ©1998, UNI/Eureka/ILS)

Let us therefore approach the throne of grace with boldness, so that we may receive mercy and find grace to help in time of need. Hebrews 4:16

> "Let Us Pray" by Steven Curtis Chapman (*Signs of Life* ©1996, EMD/Sparrow)

Thank you, gracious Father, for your patience with us. May we learn to talk with you like this all the time, that we would live our lives completely in your will. Amen

thursday

Psalm 48
Leviticus 6:14—7:21; Mark 2:1-12

_ord will not cast away his people, for his great
e's sake. 1 Samuel 12:22

"Coming Home" by Caedmon's Call
(*Caedmon's Call* ©1997, WEA/Warner)

_ if some were unfaithful? Will their faithlessness
_y the faithfulness of God? By no means!
_ans 3:3-4

"No One Loves Me Like You Do" by Jars of
Clay (*If I Left The Zoo* ©1999,
BMG/Jive/Silvertone)

_rd, we lift up your name and sing your praises
_use you are so faithful to us. Day after day you
_ for us to know you more and yet we fail you.
_h us obedience. Amen

---

friday

Psalm 49:1-12
Leviticus 7:22—8:17; Mark 2:13-28

not say, 'I am only a boy,' for you shall go to all
hom I send you, and you shall speak whatever I
mand you." Jeremiah 1:7

"The Hammer Holds" by Bebo Norman (*Ten
Thousand Days* ©1999, BMG/Brentwood)

I wrote:] "If I proclaim the gospel, this gives me
round for boasting, for an obligation is laid on
and woe to me if I do not proclaim the gospel!"
_rinthians 9:16

"What If I Stumble?" by dc Talk (*Jesus Freak*
©1995, EMD/Chordant)

we know you have chosen us to spread your
to others. Let us today be secure in the power of
Holy Spirit and share our faith. Amen

WEEK 15

▮▮▮ Psalm 49:13-20
▮▮▮ Leviticus 8:18—9:11; Mark 3:1-12

The fear of the LORD is instruction in wisdom, and humility goes before honor. Proverbs 15:33

> "Shine" by the Newsboys (*Shine...The Hits* ©2000, EMD/Sparrow)

Clothe yourselves, all of you, with humility toward one another. 1 Peter 5:5

> "Holiness" by Sonicflood (*Sonicflood* ©1999, EMD/Chordant)

Dear Lord, make us depend on your strength alone. We desire to be humble creatures. We are not worthy to be called yours, but by grace you do. Thank you. Amen

WEEK 16

 Watchword for the Week

[Jesus spoke:] "I am the good shepherd. My sheep hear my voice. I know them, and they follow me. I give them eternal life." John 10:11, 27-28

You, O LORD, are good and forgiving, abounding in steadfast love to all who call on you. Psalm 86:5

> "Love Is Different" by Caedmon's Call (*Long Line of Leavers* ©2000, BMG/Brentwood)

[Jesus Christ said:] "Ask, and it will be given you; search, and you will find; knock, and the door will be opened for you." Luke 11:9

> "Day by Day" by dc Talk (*Jesus Freak* ©1995, EMD/Chordant)

God, help us to ask your forgiveness for our sins. Allow us to bask in the shine of your unconditional love and give us the desire to continue seeking after your ways. Show us and help us know how to follow the path that is best for us in your eyes. Amen

Psalm 50:1-6

Leviticus 9:12—10:20; Mark 3:13-19

not put the LORD your God to the test.
teronomy 6:16

"Prove Me Wrong" by Caedmon's Call (*Long Line of Leavers* ©2000, BMG/Brentwood)

, however, that you have come to know God, or
er to be known by God, how can you turn back
n to the weak and beggarly elemental spirits?
tians 4:9

"Real Good Thing" by the Newsboys (*Going Public* ©1994, EMD/Sparrow)

, forgive us for doubting you and needing to see
of your power. Help us to trust your word and
comfort in your arms. Keep us from falling back
the ways we followed before we found you, and
us on the right path. Thank you for forgiving us
n we do fall into bad choices, and continue to
us out of them. Amen

Psalm 50:7-15

Leviticus 11:1-30; Mark 3:20-34

there is still a vision for the appointed time; it
ks of the end, and does not lie. Habakkuk 2:3

"Past the Edges" by Chris Rice (*Past the Edges* ©1998, Sony/Word)

us Christ spoke:] "People will come from east and
, from north and south, and will eat in the king-
of God." Luke 13:29

"Colored People" by dc Talk (*Jesus Freak* ©1995, EMD/Chordant)

us to wait patiently for your coming, God. We
forward to the time when all of your people will
ogether in one beautiful place; people of all
rs and from all places. Thank you for the promise
our kingdom. Amen

WEEK 16

■ Psalm 50:16-23
■ Leviticus 11:31—13:8; Mark 4:1-20

It is in vain that you rise up early and go late to rest, eating the bread of anxious toil; for he gives sleep to his beloved. Psalm 127:2

> "Shortstop" by Steve Taylor (*Roaring Lambs* ©2000, Squint)

[Jesus Christ said:] "But strive first for the kingdom of God and his righteousness, and all these things will be given to you as well." Matthew 6:33

> "Great Lengths" by PFR (*Great Lengths* ©1993, Chordant)

Dear God, help us to realize and believe in our head and our heart that we don't have to try to do everything alone. God, we want to give things up to you; please help us do that. Thank you so much for carrying our burdens for us and for being our truest friend. We trust you with every part of our life. Amen

WEEK 16

■ Psalm 51:1-6
■ Leviticus 13:9-46; Mark 4:21-29

I will bless you as long as I live; I will lift up my hands and call on your name. Psalm 63:4

> "And Your Praise Goes On" by Chris Rice (*Past the Edges* ©1998, Sony/Word)

With joy give thanks to the Father, who has enabled you to share in the inheritance of the saints in the light. Colossians 1:12

> "Trials Turned to Gold" by PFR (*Great Lengths* ©1993, Chordant)

God, you are an awesome God! Thank you for the many blessings you rain down on us each day. The gift of your Son can't be described it is so wonderful, but thank you for sending him to the earth. Through Jesus, we know that when we physically die we can live on forever with you in your kingdom. Help us continue to trust you each day. Amen

friday

Psalm 51:7-12
Leviticus 13:47—14:18;
ark 4:30-41

e up, come to our help. Redeem us for the sake of
ur steadfast love. Psalm 44:26

"It's You, Jesus" by PFR (*Great Lengths* ©1993,
Chordant)

when the fullness of time had come, God sent his
, born of a woman, born under the law, in order
redeem those who were under the law, so that we
ght receive adoption as children. Galatians 4:4-5

"Touch" by Delirious? (*Roaring Lambs* ©2000,
Squint)

*d, thank you for sending your Son at just the right
e to save us from our sins. Please help us through
y kind of trials we may face. We're so thankful that
u love us enough to guide us in troubling times,
en when we have brought things upon ourselves.
en*

saturday

Psalm 51:13-19
Leviticus 14:19-57; Mark 5:1-20

away the foreign gods that are among you, and
line your hearts to the LORD. Joshua 24:23

"Whatever Happened to Sin?" by Steve Taylor
(*I Want to Be a Clone* ©1983, Chordant)

know that the Son of God has come and has
en us understanding so that we may know him
o is true. 1 John 5:20

"Mind's Eye" by dc Talk (*Jesus Freak* ©1995,
EMD/Chordant)

*d, forgive us for putting some things in our life
ove you. Help us to tear down these idols we've
ilt for ourselves. We now realize that, in the end,
ese things will do nothing good for us and may
en hurt us. We know, God, that only you can fulfill
d sustain us. Help us to trust this knowledge that
u've given us, and to live by it. Amen*

WEEK 17

sunday

Watchword for the Week

If anyone is in Christ, there is a new creation: everything old has passed away; see, everything has become new! 2 Corinthians 5:17

The heart is devious above all else; it is perverse—who can understand it? I the LORD test the mind and search the heart, to give to all according to their ways, according to the fruit of their doings. Jeremiah 17:9-10

> "Mighty Good Leader" by Audio Adrenaline (*Hit Parade* ©2001, EMD/Chordant)

Therefore do not pronounce judgment before the time, before the Lord comes, who will bring to light the things now hidden in darkness and will disclose the purposes of the heart. 1 Corinthians 4:5

> "A Brand New Day" by Brad Bennett (*Songs for the Journey* ©Brad Bennett. For more information, click on www.brad-bennett.com)

God, forgive us for deviating from the path you have set before us. Keep us from temptation and from our own heart's sneaky ways. Thank you for knowing our hearts, even the bad parts, and still loving us. Forgive us for judging others. Amen

WEEK 17

monday

 Psalm 52
 Leviticus 15:1-24; Mark 5:21-43

The LORD said [to Jonah,] "Is it right for you to be angry?" Jonah 4:4

> "Parables of Grace" by Brad Bennett (*Songs for the Journey* ©Brad Bennett. For more information, click on www.brad-bennett.com)

[Jesus told the parable of the prodigal son:] "But we had to celebrate and rejoice, because this brother of yours was dead and has come to life; he was lost and has been found." Luke 15:32

> "Forgive" by Millenial Swing (*Millenial Swing* ©Servant)

God, forgive us for being so quick to anger. We lose our tempers far too easily and over simple things. Help us to be more mild-tempered, dear God. Thank you for being slow to anger when dealing with us. Also, forgive us for feeling resentful of others when they receive your grace, even if we don't think they deserve it. Put a joy in our heart for these people who, just like the prodigal son, come humbly back to you. Amen

WEEK 17

tuesday

■ Psalm 53
■ Leviticus 15:25—16:25; Mark 6:1-6

not fear, O land; be glad and rejoice, for the LORD
done great things! Joel 2:21

"Psalm" by Millenial Swing (*Millenial Swing*
©Servant)

us hold fast to the confession of our hope without
ering, for he who has promised is faithful.
rews 10:23

"Live by Faith" by Chris Rice (*Past the Edges*
©1998, Sony/Word)

, thank you for being in our lives! You have done,
continue to do, awesome things for us and we
k you for that. Help us to continue to be faithful
ou, even when we doubt or have questions.
k you for the fact that you always make yourself
wn and bring us out of doubting times. Amen

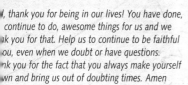

WEEK 17

wednesday

■ Psalm 54
■ Leviticus 16:26—18:5; Mark 6:7-13

hand of our God was upon us, and he delivered
Ezra 8:31

"The Hardway" by dc Talk (*Free at Last* ©1992,
EMD/Sparrow)

him we have set our hope that he will rescue us
n. 2 Corinthians 1:10b

"Valleys Fill First" by Caedmon's Call (*Long Line
of Leavers* ©2000, BMG/Brentwood)

, thank you for protecting us. You watch over us
en we are awake, when we're asleep, and even
en we don't realize you're there. Thank you for
ging us through the rough times in our lives. We
tinue to have faith that you will keep rescuing us
en we fall into hardship. Amen

WEEK 17

■ Psalm 55:1-8
■ Leviticus 18:6—19:11; Mark 6:14-29

I will turn their mourning into joy. Jeremiah 31:13

> "Good Life" by Audio Adrenaline (*Underdog*
> ©1999, EMD/Chordant)

Jesus said to [Martha,] "Did I not tell you that if you
believed, you would see the glory of God?"
John 11:40

> "Like a Child" by Jars of Clay (*Jars of Clay*
> ©1995, BMG/Jive/Silvertone)

*God, thank you for giving us a joyful heart! Though
we can't physically see you, we have faith and
believe that you are with us all the time. When there
are obstacles in our way, causing us to doubt, please
help us to still believe in you and your presence in
our life. Amen*

WEEK 17

■ Psalm 55:9-15
■ Leviticus 19:12—20:7; Mark 6:30-44

The LORD has made known his victory; he has
revealed his vindication in the sight of the nations.
Psalm 98:2

> "Big Enough" by Chris Rice (*Past the Edges*
> ©1998, Sony/Word)

All nations will come and worship before you, for your
judgments have been revealed. Revelation 15:4

> "Liquid" by Jars of Clay (*Jars of Clay* ©1995,
> BMG/Jive/Silvertone)

*God, thank you for revealing yourself to us. Help us
to know and believe that you will be victorious.
Come and claim victory over our heart, dear Lord.
Amen*

saturday

Psalm 55:16-19
Leviticus 20:8—21:12; Mark 6:45-56

Lᴏʀᴅ, do not rebuke me in your anger, or discipline
[m]e in your wrath. Psalm 6:1

"Grace of God" by PFR (*Great Lengths* ©1993,
Chordant)

God has destined us not for wrath but for obtain-
[ing] salvation through our Lord Jesus Christ, who died
[for] us, so that whether we are awake or asleep we
[may] live with him. 1 Thessalonians 5:9-10

"Incomplete" by Switchfoot (*New Way to Be
Human* ©1999, EMD/Chordant)

[Lor]d, thank you for your forgiving heart! We rarely, if
[eve]r, deserve forgiveness. Instead, we deserve to be
[pu]nished. But because you love us and Jesus died for
[us,] you don't punish us in anger. Thank you for your
[me]rcy. Please help us to grow a forgiving heart as
[wel]l. We live through your grace, but we often fail at
[sho]wing others the same love. Forgive us, and help to
[cha]nge our heart. Amen

sunday

Watchword for the Week

O sing to the Lᴏʀᴅ a new song, for
he has done marvelous things.
Psalm 98:1

God sent his angel and shut the lions' mouths so
[tha]t they would not hurt me, because I was found
[bla]meless before him. Daniel 6:22

"Message of the Cross" by Delirious? (*Cutting
Edge* ©1997, EMD/Sparrow)

[We] know that those who are born of God do not sin.
[1 Jo]hn 5:18

"Rest Easy" by Audio Adrenaline (*Hit Parade*
©2001 EMD/Chordant)

[Jes]us, your word says that if we ask anything in your
[nam]e, you will do it. You know our lives, and you
[kno]w our struggles. We know we are weak, but we are
[not] alone. In your name, Jesus, show your powerful
[gra]ce in our lives. Amen

WEEK 18

■ Psalm 55:20-23
■ Leviticus 21:13—22:16; Mark 7:1-7

It is I, announcing vindication, mighty to save.
Isaiah 63:1

> "Consume Me" by dc Talk (*Supernatural*
> ©1998, EMD/Virgin)

To this day I have had help from God, and so I stand
here, testifying to both small and great. Acts 26:22

> "Masquerade" by Reality Check (*Reality Check*
> ©1997, Chordant)

*Holy Spirit, work from our insides out. Take our
hearts and change them. Let them fall deep into your
arms of love. Consume our thoughts, our hearts, and
our actions. We know that when our hearts are
changed, it shows outwardly. When people see our
lives, let them see you. Amen*

WEEK 18

■ Psalm 56:1-8
■ Leviticus 22:17—23:21; Mark 7:8-23

My lips will shout for joy when I sing praises to you;
my soul also, which you have rescued. Psalm 71:23

> "What If I Stumble?" by dc Talk (*Jesus Freak*
> ©1995, EMD/Chordant)

In [Jesus Christ] we have redemption through his
blood, the forgiveness of our trespasses, according to
the riches of his grace. Ephesians 1:7

> "Carry Me High" by Rebecca St. James (*God*
> ©1996, EMD/Chordant)

*Sometimes expectations from others are hard to
meet, but Jesus, your grace flows like a river through
eternity. We are children, learning to walk in your
ways. When we fall, pick us up. Do not let people
judge our fall. Instead, let them see you work through
it all. Amen*

WEEK 18

wednesday

Psalm 56:9-13
Leviticus 23:22—24:9; Mark 7:24-37

the command of the LORD they would camp, and
the command of the LORD they would set out.
umbers 9:23

"Dive" by Steven Curtis Chapman (*Speechless*
©1999, EMD/Sparrow)

y sheep hear my voice. I know them, and they
low me. I give them eternal life. John 10:27-28

"Like a Child" by Jars of Clay (*Jars of Clay*
©1995, BMG/Jive/Silvertone)

day is the day, Lord God, we stand in your pres-
ce, broken, with faith left standing. We surrender
ho we are and what we have into your arms. Burn a
ssionate fire in us, O God, that we may seek your
orious face every day. Amen

WEEK 18

thursday

Psalm 57:1-6
Leviticus 24:10—25:17; Mark 8:1-13

e shall be the one of peace. Micah 5:5a

"Everybody Needs Love" by Seven Day Jesus
(*Seven Day Jesus* ©1998, EMD/Chordant)

ace I leave with you; my peace I give to you. I do
t give to you as the world gives. Do not let your
arts be troubled, and do not let them be afraid.
hn 14:27

"I Could Sing of Your Love Forever" by
Delirious? (*Cutting Edge* ©1997, EMD/Sparrow)

d, your everlasting love for us is so amazing. It
reshes us to see you provide for even the smallest
eds of my life. The way you care when no one else
tices brings us to say thank you. Amen

WEEK 18

Psalm 57:7-11
Leviticus 25:18-55; Mark 8:14-21

The sacrifice acceptable to God is a broken spirit; a broken and contrite heart, O God, you will not despise. Psalm 51:17

"Pour Me Out" by PFR (*Late Great PFR* ©1997, Chordant)

[Jesus said:] "Those who are well have no need of a physician, but those who are sick; I have come to call not the righteous but sinners." Mark 2:17

"The Happy Song" by Delirious? (*Cutting Edge* ©1997, EMD/Sparrow)

Holy Spirit, humble our hearts to see you move through our lives. We want to see the way that you've blessed us, so we can praise you with fountains of joy spilling over in our hearts. Thank you, Jesus, for giving us your infinite treasure of love. Amen

WEEK 18

Psalm 58
Leviticus 26:1-35; Mark 8:22-38

You are my witnesses, says the LORD. Isaiah 43:10

"What I Cannot Earn" by The Normals (*Better Than This* ©1998, Chordant)

[Jesus prayed for the disciples:] Sanctify them in the truth; your word is truth. As you have sent me into the world, so I have sent them into the world. John 17:17-18

"Better Is One Day" by Passion Worship Band (*Passion: Better Is One Day* ©2000 EMD/Sparrow)

Jesus, take all of us, in every way. We want to be closer to you. You are our shepherd, and we are your sheep. Guide us in your truth. To be with you means more than anything the world has to offer. We love you. Amen

sunday

Watchword for the Week

Blessed be God, because he has not rejected my prayer or removed his steadfast love from me. Psalm 66:20

...eph reassured [his brothers], speaking kindly to ...m. Genesis 50:21

"Each Other" by Skillet (*Invincible* ©2000, Ardent Music)

... not repay anyone evil for evil, but take thought for ...at is noble in the sight of all. Romans 12:17

"Check217" by PAX217 (*Twoseventeen* ©2000, ForeFront)

...Lord our God, you forgive us even as we ignore and ...ect you. May our love for you be strong enough to ...me together as one family, forgiving each other as ... fall, hurt each other, and feel weak at times. We ... all created equal not perfect, with Christ Jesus as ... only redemptive claim. Amen

monday

Psalm 59:1-9
Leviticus 26:36—27:15; Mark 9:1-10

... the LORD your God is God of gods and LORD of ...ds, the great God, mighty and awesome, who is ...t partial and takes no bribe. Deuteronomy 10:17

"There Is Only You" by Small Town Poets (*Listen Closely* ©1998, Ardent)

... from him and through him and to him are all ...ngs. To him be the glory forever! Romans 11:36

"Love" by Imagine This (*Love* ©1995, Brentwood)

...ther, the source of all things, there are so many ...erests to us in this world; are we dumb enough to ... drawn into them, can we be brave enough to run ...ay, run to you? Open our eyes that we may see ...u standing there, as you truly are everywhere. ...men

WEEK 19

■ Psalm 59:10-17
■ Leviticus 27:16-34; Numbers 1:1-16;
Mark 9:11-29

The hope of the righteous ends in gladness.
Proverbs 10:28

> "Don't Worry" by Crystal Lewis (*The Bride*
> ©1993, Metro One)

Christ was faithful over God's house as a son, and we
are his house if we hold firm the confidence and the
pride that belong to hope. Hebrews 3:6

> "We Will Embrace Your Move" by Darrell Evans
> (*Dove Award Worship* ©2000, Sony/Word)

*Great Father above, we come again—yes, those who
worry about every decision and move that we make,
about tomorrow, and what's to come. We ask you to
help us learn to stop this madness and focus on you
in heaven. As you prepare us for your house, may we
be active and confident in the way you are moving.
Amen*

WEEK 19

■ Psalm 60
■ Numbers 1:17-54; Mark 9:30-37

Naaman said, "Your servant will no longer offer burnt
offering or sacrifice to any god except the LORD.
2 Kings 5:17

> "Eternal Lifestyle" by All Together Separate (*All
> Together Separate* ©1999, Ardent)

[Paul wrote:] "I appeal to you therefore, brothers and
sisters, by the mercies of God, to present your bodies
as a living sacrifice, holy and acceptable to God,
which is your spiritual worship." Romans 12:1

> "Daniel" by Ffh (*Found a Place* ©2000,
> Essential)

*Our Lord, with all the things in this world we feel
that we need, help us to make our sacrifice to you be
more than just some money here, a little time there,
a hello now and then. Help us put aside our own
desires, and put all our resources toward you. Amen*

Psalm 61

Numbers 2:1-34; Mark 9:38-50

...day the LORD commands his steadfast love, and at ...ht his song is with me, a prayer to the God of my ... Psalm 42:8

"My Hope Is You" by Third Day (*Conspiracy* #5 ©1997, BMG/Jive/Silvertone)

...y without ceasing, give thanks in all circumstances; ...this is the will of God in Christ Jesus for you. ...hessalonians 5:17-18

"How Could I But Love You" by Tommy Walker (*Never Gonna Stop* ©2000, Integrity)

...d of all creation, you are faithfully with us day-by- ... and night-by-night. May all that we do reflect ...r love that has been shown to us. What else can ...do except be a living testimony and follow you? ...y all that we do help others to see the love of our ...ior. Amen

Psalm 62

Numbers 3:1-26; Mark 10:1-12

...e LORD has done great things for us, and we ...iced. Psalm 126:3

"God Is Good" by Scarecrow and Tinmen (*Superhero* ©2000, Organic)

...ving been made perfect, Jesus Christ became the ...rce of eternal salvation for all who obey him. ...brews 5:9

"I Believe It" by the Kry (*What About Now* ©1996, Freedom)

...esome God, with awesome works, we are in awe ...t Jesus shared our human existence and can offer ...eternal salvation. You show us life every day ...luding the sun rising and setting. May we rejoice ...d shout aloud of your goodness and great works. ...p us obey your word. Amen

WEEK 19

■ Psalm 63
■ Numbers 3:27—4:11; Mark 10:13-31

Sing for joy, O heavens, and exult, O earth; break forth, O mountains, into singing! For the LORD has comforted his people, and will have compassion on his suffering ones. Isaiah 49:13

> "Did You Feel the Mountains Tremble?" by Delirious? (*Cutting Edge* ©1997, EMD/Sparrow)

The Son of Man came to seek out and to save the lost. Luke 19:10

> "Willow Tree" by Plumb (*Plumb* ©1997, Brentwood)

O Lord of heaven and earth, your love for your children who are lost is unmeasurable. You know precisely where and how to make yourself known to us. We could give you directions, but they would be limited by our life view. You not only know where we are and how to get here, you see the big picture and truly know what is best. We await your timing. Amen

WEEK 20

Watchword for the Week
[Christ said:] "When I am lifted up from the earth, I will draw all people to myself." John 12:32

Surely it was for my welfare that I had great bitterness; but you have held back my life from the pit of destruction, for you have cast all my sins behind your back. Isaiah 38:17

> "Why Don't You Look into Jesus?" by Holy Soldier (*Promise Man* ©1995, ForeFront)

Jesus said to her, "Woman, where are they? Has no one condemned you?" She said, "No one, sir." And Jesus said, "Neither do I condemn you. Go your way, and from now on do not sin again." John 8:10-11

> "Beautiful to Me" by Don Francisco (*Beautiful to Me* ©Ministry Music)

Dear Savior, our sins are so nasty and we are so ashamed but still, you wait and are ready to forgive us. May we daily look to you, ask forgiveness and walk away from our sins leaving them behind—just as you place our sins behind not to look at them again. We are forever grateful. Amen

monday

Psalm 64
Numbers 4:12-49; Mark 10:32-45

...e ponder your steadfast love, O God, in the midst ...your temple. Psalm 48:9

"Surrender" by Glenn Kaiser (*All My Days* ©1993, Grrr)

...ter and John went to the temple to pray. Acts 3:1

"Hungry (falling on my knees)" by Kathryn Scott (*Hungry* ©2001, EMD/Chordant)

...need of strength, dear Lord, you give us everything ...d more. May we take time out this day, every ...y—even three times or continually during the ...y—to kneel down, surrender and praise your amaz-...g grace. For without you, what would become of ...? Amen

tuesday

Psalm 65:1-8
Numbers 5:1-31; Mark 10:46-52

...ur steps are made firm by the LORD, when he ...lights in our way; though we stumble, we shall not ...l headlong, for the LORD holds us by the hand. ...alm 37:23-24

"What If I Stumble?" by dc Talk (*Jesus Freak* ©1995, ForeFront/EMD/Chordant)

...sus Christ said:] They will never perish. No one will ...atch them out of my hand. John 10:28

"He Will Always Be There" by the Supertones (*Adventures of the O.C. Supertones* ©1996, Tooth & Nail)

...rd, help us to seek your will before compromising, ...mping into things on our own, and sinking. For we ...d in your Word that you know your sheep and ...at you will protect us. We can anticipate suffering, ...t no one can take away our eternal life that we ...ve with you. Thank you! Amen

WEEK 20

■ Psalm 65:9-13
■ Numbers 6:1-27; Mark 11:1-11

I will punish the people who rest complacently on their dregs, those who say in their hearts, "The LORD will not do good, nor will he do harm."
Zephaniah 1:12

> "Skip to the End" by Mukala (*Fiction* ©1998, Essential)

If you think you are standing, watch out that you do not fall. 1 Corinthians 10:12

> "We Are Not as Strong as We Think We Are" by Rich Mullins (*Songs* ©1996, Reunion)

Almighty God, you are so loving, yet so evidently strong, shaping our lives and the world around us. May we be instructed to start over again by reading the end of your book first, and see that you have the power and the judgment call. Amen

WEEK 20

■ Psalm 66:1-7
■ Numbers 7:1-35; Mark 11:12-26

Help us, O God of our salvation, for the glory of your name; deliver us, and forgive our sins, for your name's sake. Psalm 79:9

> "Above All" by Lenny LeBlanc (*Above All* ©1999, Integrity)

[The Angel spoke to Joseph,] "Mary will bear a son, and you are to name him Jesus, for he will save his people from their sins." Matthew 1:21

> "He Will Come and Save You" (*America's Newest Praise and Worship* ©1999, BMG/Brentwood)

We pray for all those whose lives are frightened, shattered, and out of order. Help them to know the Lord saves, for we cannot save ourselves from our own sinful nature. Jesus, only you could remember us and purge our sins through your righteousness and crucifixion. We love you, Lord. Amen

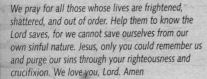

friday

■ Psalm 66:8-15
■ Numbers 7:36-71;
Mark 11:27—12:12

s for me, I said in my prosperity, "I shall never be
oved." By your favor, O LORD, you had established
e as a strong mountain; you hid your face; I was
smayed. Psalm 30:6-7

| "Hypocrite" by the World Wide Message Tribe
(*Heatseeker* ©1998, Warner Brothers)

t three o'clock Jesus cried out with a loud voice,
Eloi, Eloi, lema sabachthani?" which means, "My
od, my God, why have you forsaken me?"
Mark 15:34

| "No One's Ever Died for Me Before" by John
Elefante (*Windows of Heaven* ©1995, Word)

ord, sometimes we think we're doing so well keep-
g the faith and your commands. Then we see that
e're really doing things that we don't want to do:
eing passive about things that we should stand up
r and holding onto material items too closely.
hange our hearts as you guide us out of this self-
liance and temporary separation from you. Amen

---

saturday

■ Psalm 66:16-20
■ Numbers 7:72—8:4; Mark 12:13-17

emember your congregation, which you acquired
ng ago, which you redeemed to be the tribe of your
eritage. Psalm 74:2

| "Big Fish" by Ffh (*I Want to Be Like You*
©1998, Brentwood/Benson)

Christ we have also obtained an inheritance.
hesians 1:11

| "This Is My Destiny" by Dennis Jernigan (*This Is
My Destiny* ©1998, Shepherds Heart)

aise you almighty God, for you remember us and
e there to rescue us when you could just throw us
t to dry. We have been cleansed with a new life as
u call us your own and share with us eternal life
gether, a true fortune. Praise you forever and ever.
men

WEEK 21

Watchword for the Week
Not by might, nor by power, but by my spirit, says the LORD of hosts. Zechariah 4:6

The LORD will guide you continually, and satisfy your needs in parched places. Isaiah 58:11

"Take My Life" (*WoW Worship—Today's 30 Most Powerful Worship Songs* ©1999, Sony/Word)

When the Spirit of truth comes, he will guide you into all the truth. John 16:13

"Lean On" by Rebecca St. James (*Transform* ©2000, Up in the Mix Music)

Lord, remind us today of your loving kindness and show us your will today. Teach us to be thankful for the difficult situations in our lives. We know that in every situation, you are present. We trust the plans you have for our lives. Show us where you are working and show us how you want us to be used to further your kingdom. Amen

WEEK 21

■■■ Psalm 67
■■■ Numbers 8:5—9:14; Mark 12:18-34

My house shall be called a house of prayer for all peoples. Isaiah 56:7

"Pray" by The Echoing Green (*Defend Your Joy* ©1996, EMI)

Then the master said to the slave, "Go out into the roads and lanes, and compel people to come in, so that my house may be filled." Luke 14:23

"Shaken" by Rachael Lampa (*Live for You* ©2000, Word)

Father, there are people in our lives that do not know who you are or do not understand your truth. Give us opportunities to share the message of your love and grace and give us boldness to speak the truth in love. Use us as your divine instruments and make clear for us the words that you want us to speak. Amen

tuesday

- Psalm 68:1-6
- Numbers 9:15—10:36; Mark 12:35-44

Be mindful of your mercy, O Lord, and of your stead-
ast love, for they have been from of old.
Psalm 25:6

> "Merciful" by Rebecca St. James (*Transform*
> ©2000, Up in the Mix)

In this is love, not that we loved God but that he
loved us and sent his Son to be the atoning sacrifice
or our sins. 1 John 4:10

> "Enter Love" by The Echoing Green (*Defend
> Your Joy* ©1996, EMI)

Dear God, thank you for loving us and for sending
your Son, Jesus, to die for our sins. Thank you for
your mercy and forgiveness. Your unconditional love
is incomprehensible. Help us to love others with your
kind of love. Help us to show the same mercy and
grace to the people that are a part of our lives. Amen

---

wednesday

- Psalm 68:7-18
- Numbers 11:1-35; Mark 13:1-13

Do not be exceedingly angry, O Lord, and do not
remember iniquity forever. Now consider, we are all
your people. Isaiah 64:9

> "Speechless" by Steven Curtis Chapman
> (*Speechless* ©1999, Sparrow)

Forgive us our sins, for we ourselves forgive everyone
indebted to us. Luke 11:4

> "The Prayer Anthem" by Carman (*Mission 3:16*
> ©1998, EMD/Chordant)

Lord, purify our hearts. Forgive us for the things in
our lives that we secretly keep hidden from the
world. You, Lord, see and know all the areas of sin in
our lives, hidden and obvious. We confess these areas
to you, Lord, and thank you that you remember our
sins no more. Amen

WEEK 21

■ Psalm 68:19-27
■ Numbers 12:1—13:16;
Mark 13:14-27

Micaiah said, "As the LORD lives, whatever my God says, that I will speak." 2 Chronicles 18:13

> "Bought with the Blood" by Ray Boltz (*Allegiance* ©1994, Word)

[Jesus said:] "I have not spoken on my own, but the Father who sent me has himself given me a commandment about what to say and what to speak." John 12:49

> "People of God" by Carman (*Mission 3:16* ©1998, EMD/Chordant)

Watch our words today, Lord. There are times when we hurt others with what we say. Bind our tongues from speaking too quickly or from saying something that might damage someone's heart. Keep our minds pure from thoughts that do not glorify you. May our thoughts be of your Word. Transform our tongues to speak what glorifies you. Amen

WEEK 21

■ Psalm 68:28-35
■ Numbers 13:17-33; Mark 13:28-37

Reuben said to [his brothers], "Shed no blood." Genesis 37:22

> "One More Broken Heart" by Point of Grace (*Rarities and Remixes* ©2000, Sony/Word)

Be merciful, just as your Father is merciful. Luke 6:36

> "At Your Mercy" by Kathy Troccoli (*Corner of Eden* ©1998, Reunion)

Dear Father, we want others to see that we love you. We want our actions and words to line up with your Word. We don't want the things that we say and the things that we do to contradict each other. Lord, we want you to be the standard by which we measure our lives. Thank you for your direction and perfect mercy. Amen

WEEK 21

■ Psalm 69:1-12
  Numbers 14:1-45; Mark 14:1-11

...nder true judgments, show kindness and mercy to
...e another. Zechariah 7:9

| "Mercy Came Running" by Phillips, Craig, and
| Dean (*Favorite Songs of All* ©1998,
| EMD/Chordant)

...ssed are the merciful, for they will receive mercy.
...atthew 5:7

| "Above All Things" by Rebecca St. James
| (*Rebecca St. James* ©1994, Chordant)

...rd, forgive us for judging others based on what we
...e and hear. Only you, Lord, can see into the hearts
...every human being. Help us to look at each person
...a child of God, who you fashioned together with a
...ecific purpose. We want to value others as you do,
...d. Amen

WEEK 22

sunday

Watchword for the Week
Holy, holy, holy is the LORD of hosts;
the whole earth is full of his glory.
Isaiah 6:3

...side in this land as an alien, and I will be with you
...d bless you. Genesis 26:3

| "Agnus Dei" by Michael W. Smith (*Go West
| Young Man* ©1990, Reunion)

...en the king will say to those at his right hand,
...ome, you that are blessed by my Father, inherit the
...gdom prepared for you ...for I was a stranger and
...u welcomed me." Matthew 25:34-35

| "The Great Divide" by Point of Grace (*Rarities
| and Remixes* ©2000, Sony/Word)

...rd, our lives are so short. Help us be witnesses of
...e gospel of Jesus Christ. Bring us opportunities to
...are the message of salvation through faith in Jesus
...h our family, friends, coworkers, and strangers. We
...truly blessed because of your presence in our lives,
...rd. Give us the strength to pass that on. Amen

WEEK 22

■ **Psalm 69:13-21**
■ **Numbers 15:1-31; Mark 14:12-31**

So they read from the book, from the law of God, with interpretation. They gave the sense, so that the people understood the reading. Nehemiah 8:8

> "I Will Follow Christ" by Clay Crosse (*I Surrender All* ©1999, Word)

Let the elders who rule well be considered worthy of double honor, especially those who labor in preaching and teaching. 1 Timothy 5:17

> "Doubly Good to You" by Amy Grant (*Straight Ahead* ©1984, Myrrh)

God, we want to be servants who are obedient to your Word like Nehemiah and we want to use the gifts you have given us to further your kingdom. Reveal to us new insights as we read and learn your holy Word. Fill our minds with understanding and touch our hearts with your everlasting love, joy, and patience. Amen

WEEK 22

■ **Psalm 69:22-29**
■ **Numbers 15:32—16:27; Mark 14:32-42**

I will look to the LORD, I will wait for the God of my salvation; my God will hear me. Micah 7:7

> "Father I Adore You" (*Songs 4 Worship: Be Glorified* ©2001, WEA/Time-Life)

For everyone who asks receives, and everyone who searches finds, and for everyone who knocks, the door will be opened. Luke 11:10

> "People Get Ready" by Crystal Lewis (*Beauty for Ashes* ©1996, Sony/Word)

Father, God, thank you for the hope you have put in our hearts. There is nothing this world could give us that even comes close to you and the blessing you have given us. Thank you for sending Jesus to die for us, sinners, now saved by grace. Thank you for standing beside us and walking this life with us. Amen

WEEK 22

Psalm 69:30-36

Numbers 16:28—17:13;
Mark 14:43-52

you obey my voice and keep my covenant, you
all be my treasured possession out of all the
oples. Exodus 19:5

"I Pledge Allegiance to the Lamb" by Ray Boltz
(*Allegiance* ©1994, Sony/Word)

sus Christ said:] "This is my commandment, that
u love one another as I have loved you."
hn 15:12

"Day of Freedom" by Rachael Lampa (*Live for
You* ©2000, Sony/Word)

rd, your love crosses all social, racial, economic,
d family barriers. It is bigger than any worldly
ssession, idea, dream, or invention. Your love can
ly be duplicated and passed on through a
ationship with Jesus. Teach us how to cross the
rriers that hold us back from sharing your message
love. Amen

WEEK 22

Psalm 70

Numbers 18:1-24; Mark 14:53-65

e LORD is merciful and gracious, slow to anger and
ounding in steadfast love. Psalm 103:8

"God Loves You" by Rachael Lampa (*Live for
You* ©2000, Sony/Word)

ay mercy, peace, and love be yours in abundance.
de 2:2

"Shine" by Newsboys (*Going Public* ©1994,
EMD/Sparrow)

ly Lord, there are many times when we are beaten
wn by life's weight and it is easy for us to take our
es off you. In those times you gently remind us that
u are always watching us and waiting for us to
ok to you for hope, wisdom, and direction. You,
d, hear and answer our prayers. Thank you. Amen

WEEK 22

■ Psalm 71:1-8
■ Numbers 18:25—19:22;
Mark 14:66-72

Then Moses stretched out his hand over the sea. The
LORD drove the sea back by a strong east wind.
Exodus 14:21

> "Great God" by Carman (*Standard* ©1993,
> EMD/Sparrow)

By faith the people passed through the Red Sea as if it
were dry land. Hebrews 11:29

> "God" by Rebecca St. James (*God* ©1996,
> EMD/Chordant)

*God, your awesome power is beyond words. Nothing
can match it and time cannot capture it. You are the
beginning and the end. You are the God of all creation. You are awe inspiring, wonderful, all knowing,
and full of mercy, compassion, and love, for all who
believe in your name. We love you, Lord, and we
praise you, Most High God. Amen*

WEEK 22

■ Psalm 71:9-18
■ Numbers 20:1—21:9; Mark 15:1-20

If your presence will not go, do not carry us up from
here. Exodus 33:15

> "Prepare Ye the Way" by Caedmon's Call (*Long
> Line of Leavers* ©2000, BMG/Brentwood)

Looking to Jesus, the pioneer and perfecter of our
faith. Hebrews 12:2

> "My Will" by dc Talk (*Exodus* ©1998,
> Sony/Word)

*Dear heavenly Father, teach us to look to you when
we feel alone. We know you are always with us but
sometimes we forget. As we seek to love you more,
may we feel your hand in our lives. Amen*

WEEK 23

sunday

Watchword for the Week

Christ spoke to his disciples: Whoever listens to you, listens to me, and whoever rejects you, rejects me. Luke 10:16

u are] the hope of Israel and its savior in time of uble. Jeremiah 14:8

"Grace" by Jars of Clay (*If I Left the Zoo* ©1999, BMG/Jive/Silvertone)

w may our Lord Jesus Christ himself and God our her who loved us and through grace gave us eternal mfort and good hope, comfort your hearts and ngthen them in every good work and word. hessalonians 2:16-17

"His Grace Is Sufficient" by Jennifer Knapp (*Kansas* ©1998, EMD/Chordant)

rd, your grace is amazing. Days when the world ms to fall apart, you rescue us with your free gift of e. Thank you for loving us so much, right here, right ere we are. You are all we need. Amen

---

WEEK 23

monday

■ Psalm 71:19-24
■ Numbers 21:10—22:6;
ark 15:21-32

shall judge between the nations...they shall beat ir swords into plowshares and their spears into ning hooks. Isaiah 2:4

"The Heart of Worship" by Sonicflood (*Sonicflood* ©1999, EMD/Chordant)

d is not a God of disorder, but of peace. orinthians 14:33

"Peace" by Jennifer Knapp (*Lay It Down* ©2000, EMD/Chordant)

at God, we know you create peace in disorder. ase teach us to be effective servants. Bless our ds and our work, as we aim to shine your light to world. Through our work, may we worship your e. Amen

WEEK 23

■■■ Psalm 72:1-11
■■■ Numbers 22:7-41; Mark 15:33-47

When they call to me, I will answer them.
Psalm 91:15

> "Like a Child" by Jars of Clay (*Jars of Clay*
> ©1995, BMG/Jive/Silvertone)

[Jesus Christ says] "If you abide in me and my words
abide in you, ask for whatever you wish, and it will be
done for you." John 15:7

> "Take You at Your Word" by Avalon (*In a
> Different Light* ©1999, EMD/Sparrow)

*Lord, you're the best listener. You listen to us when
we ramble on, when we are afraid and scared. With a
subtle touch, we know you are there, listening to
every word. Thank you for answering our calls...no
matter when we call on you. Amen*

WEEK 23

■■■ Psalm 72:12-20
■■■ Numbers 23:1-30; Mark 16:1-13

You, O LORD, are a shield around me, my glory, and
the one who lifts up my head. Psalm 3:3

> "This Mystery" by Nichole Nordeman (*This
> Mystery* ©2000, EMD/Sparrow)

The God of all grace, who has called you to his
eternal glory in Christ, will himself restore, support,
strengthen, and establish you. 1 Peter 5:10

> "My Refuge" by Sonicflood (*Sonicflood* ©1998,
> EMD/Chordant)

*Wrap your arms around us, for you are our strong
Father. Your body shields, protects, and strengthens
us. Again today, Lord, restore our souls. Make our
actions more like yours. Develop our character and
establish us in your word. Amen*

WEEK 23

thursday

Psalm 73:1-12
Numbers 24:1—25:18;
Mark 16:14-20; Luke 1:1-4

...ose gathered in from the lands, from the east and
...om the west, from the north and from the south: let
...em thank the LORD for his steadfast love, and for his
...onderful works to humankind. Psalm 107:3, 8

> "Thankful" by Caedmon's Call (*40 Acres*
> ©1999, BMG/Brentwood)

...sus prayed for his disciples: "Father, I ask not only
...behalf of these but also on behalf of those who
...lieve in me through their word, that they may all be
...e." John 17:20-21

> "Hard to Get" by Rich Mullins and the
> Ragamuffin Band (*Jesus Record* ©1998,
> Reunion)

...ving Father, you love isn't just for our friends and
...mily; it's for all people. You have a heart for the
...tions. Lord, give us opportunities to share your
...spel of love with them. Grant that one day we may
...orship you with the multitude of believers. Amen

WEEK 23

friday

Psalm 73:13-20
Numbers 26:1-24; Luke 1:5-25

...od is my helper; the LORD is the upholder of my life.
...alm 54:4

> "Small Enough" by Nichole Nordeman with
> Fernando Ortega (*This Mystery* ©2000,
> EMD/Sparrow)

...hen the man heard that Jesus had come from Judea
...Galilee, he went and begged him to come down
...d heal his son, for he was at the point of death.
...hn 4:47

> "Reach Out to Me" by Michael W. Smith (*This
> Is Your Time* ©1999, Reunion)

...rd you are our helper, healer, and Savior. We are so
...ak and feeble, but you always reach down to pick
...up, brush off the dirt, and put us on our feet
...ain. We are so grateful that you are there, holding
...r hands and watching over us. Amen

WEEK 23

▨▨▨ Psalm 73:21-28
▨▨▨ Numbers 26:25-56; Luke 1:26-38

The LORD heard our voice and saw our affliction, our toil and our oppression. Deuteronomy 26:7

> "All That I Have Sown" by Bebo Norman (*Big Blue Sky* ©2001, Reunion)

The disciples woke Jesus up, saying: "Lord, save us!" And he said to them, "Why are you afraid, you of little faith?" Matthew 8:25-26

> "Prove Me Wrong" by Caedmon's Call (*Long Line of Leavers* ©2000, BMG/Brentwood)

When we are drowning in the world's suffering, you hear our calls for help, merciful God. You see our pain and come to alleviate it. Let us not forget that you are always there and that by our faith you will rescue us. Amen

WEEK 24

Watchword for the Week
Christ said: "Come to me all who labor and are heavy laden; I will refresh you." Matthew 11:28

The LORD has sent me to comfort all who mourn. Isaiah 61:1-2

> "Glory Baby" by Watermark (*All Things New* ©2000, Rocketown/Word)

Mary stood weeping outside the tomb. Jesus said to her, "Woman, why are you weeping? Whom do you seek?" John 20:11, 15

> "He's My Son" by Mark Schultz (*Mark Schultz* ©2000, Sony/Word)

Comfort us, Lord Jesus. Take the sorrow and the fear we feel and replace it with your overflowing peace. You, Lord, are bigger than our greatest pains. Teach us to seek you in times of trouble and not to turn away from you. Amen

WEEK 24

Psalm 74:1-9

Numbers 26:57—27:23; Luke 1:39-45

...will remember my covenant with you in the days of your youth, and I will establish with you an everlasting covenant. Ezekiel 16:60

"The Ninety and Nine" by Andrew Peterson (*Carried Along* ©2000, BMG/Brentwood)

...Christ Jesus you are all children of God through faith. As many of you as were baptized into Christ have clothed yourselves with him. Galatians 3:26-27

"Children of the Burning Heart" by Steven Curtis Chapman (*Signs of Life* ©1996, EMD/Sparrow)

...sus Christ, Lord of all, we are so grateful that we are your children. When you established a covenant with our ancestors, you promised to love their children for all generations to come. Thank you for this continued promise and the comfort we feel knowing you will always love us. Amen

WEEK 24

Psalm 74:10-17

Numbers 28:1—29:6; Luke 1:46-56

...your distress, when all these things have happened to you in time to come, you will return to the LORD your God and heed him. Deuteronomy 4:30

"Say You Need Love" by the Newsboys (*Love Liberty Disco* ©1999, EMD/Sparrow)

...esus Christ says] "I have come to call the sinners to repentance and not the righteous." Luke 5:32

"Come" by Nichole Nordeman with Fernando Ortega (*This Mystery* ©2000, EMD/Sparrow)

...erciful God, time after time we mess up, yet you ...ll us back to you. Take our distress, sins, and anger ...d change our hearts to one that worships you only. ...u are the Lord God of all of creation and we want ...follow you. Amen

WEEK 24

Psalm 74:18-23
Numbers 29:7-40; Luke 1:57-66

One who rules over people justly, ruling in the fear of God, is like the light of morning, like the sun rising on a cloudless morning. 2 Samuel 23:3-4

> "Heroes" by Justin McRoberts (*Father* ©2000, Chordant)

[Jesus spoke to the disciples] "You know that the rulers of the Gentiles lord it over them, and their great ones are tyrants over them. It will not be so among you; but whoever wishes to be great among you must be your servant." Matthew 20:25-26

> "Rachel Delevoryas" by Randy Stonehill (*Our Recollections* ©1996, Word)

Lord, teach us that to be leaders we must first be servants. Let us not get so caught up in the power of our positions that we forget when are dealing with people. Make us attentive to the needs of those around us and keep us in tune with you. Amen

WEEK 24

Psalm 75
Numbers 30:1—31:12; Luke 1:67-80

Even heaven and the highest heaven cannot contain you—much less this house that I have built! 1 Kings 8:27

> "You're Everywhere" by Third Day (*Offerings: A Worship Album* ©2000, BMG/Brentwood)

No one has ever seen God; if we love one another, God lives in us, and his love is perfected in us. 1 John 4:12

> "Live by Faith" by Chris Rice (*Past the Edges* ©1998, Sony/Word)

Awesome God, you are bigger than we can imagine. Though we can never see you, we know you are there. Thank you for those special moments when we truly feel your arms around us. Let us share our awe and your love with others. Amen

friday

■ Psalm 76
    Numbers 31:13-47; Luke 2:1-20

he place where it was said to them, "You are not
people," it shall be said to them, "Children of the
g God." Hosea 1:10

"Fingerprints of God" by Steven Curtis
Chapman (*Speechless* ©1999, EMD/Sparrow)

what love the Father has given us: that we shall
alled children of God. 1 John 3:1

"Remember Me" by Mark Schultz (*Mark
Schultz* ©2000, Sony/Word)

day we wear many hats. We're sisters, brothers,
nds, daughters, sons, employees, and students.
the most important role we play in life is as chil-
 of God. Lord, let us recognize that your love
s our life meaning. Thank you for loving us.
en

---

saturday

    Psalm 77:1-9
■ Numbers 31:48—32:27; Luke 2:21-32

n Abram said to Lot, "Let there be no strife
ween you and me, and between your herders and
herders, for we are kindred." Genesis 13:8

"Eileen's Song" by Burlap to Cashmere
(*Anybody Out There?* ©1997, UNI/Eureka/ILS)

 with one another in love. Ephesians 4:2

"More Than You'll Ever Know" by Watermark
(*All Things New* ©2000, Rocketown/Word)

 Lord, you command us to love one another, yet
 fail you time and again. Please forgive the harsh
ds we have spoken and the unkind thoughts we
 thought. Give us the patience and courage to
 all your children. Amen

WEEK 25

Watchword for the Week
The Son of Man has come to seek and save the lost. Luke 19:10

In God we have boasted continually, and we will give thanks to your name forever. Psalm 44:8

"The Walk" by Steven Curtis Chapman (*Signs of Life* ©1996, EMD/Sparrow)

[The disciples] returned to Jerusalem with great joy and they were continually in the temple blessing God. Luke 24:52-53

"All Things Are Possible" by Hillsongs (*Shout to the Lord—Platinum Collection* ©2000, Sony/Word)

Lord, we often speak of your love. We often talk about how our peers should act. Help us to speak through actions, and make our words be true. Help us to show your love through all that we say and all that we do. Lord, help us not to harp on others, but to help them understand your unconditional love. Amen

WEEK 25

■ Psalm 77:10-15
■ Numbers 32:28—33:9; Luke 2:33-40

I lie down and sleep; I wake again, for the LORD sustains me. Psalm 3:5

"The Call" by Anointed (*Call* ©1995, Sony/Word)

The very night before Herod was going to bring him out, Peter, bound with two chains, was sleeping between two soldiers. Suddenly an angel of the LORD appeared, woke him and said: "Get up quickly." And the chains fell off his wrists. Acts 12:6-7

"Revolution" by Kirk Franklin (*Nu Nation Project* ©1998, UNI/Gospocentric)

Great Creator, you set us free. You set us free from our transgressions, from our sins and from our troubles. Continue to set us free, Lord. It is by you that we receive freedom. Amen

tuesday

Psalm 77:16-20
Numbers 33:10-56; Luke 2:41-52

...hold me according to your promise, that I may live,
...d let me not be put to shame in my hope.
...alm 119:116

"Yes, I Believe in God" by Rebecca St. James
(*Whatever It Takes—She Said Yes* ©2000,
WEA/New Haven)

...u have been born anew, not of perishable but of
...perishable seed, through the living and enduring
...rd of God. 1 Peter 1:23

"Believer" (*Left Behind* soundtrack ©2000,
Reunion)

...ther, sometimes having faith is scary. We do not
...ow what speaking of your love will bring. Help us
... spread the word of your love without fear of
...rsecution. Help us to share your love with all the
...rld. Finally, help us to share the eternal life that
... all have when we choose to walk with you. Amen

wednesday

Psalm 78:1-8
Numbers 34:1-29; Luke 3:1-17

...e light of the moon will be like the light of the sun,
...d the light of the sun will be sevenfold on the day
...en the LORD binds up the injuries of his people, and
...als the wounds of his people. Isaiah 30:26

"Sometimes He Calms the Storm" by Scott
Krippayne (*Wild Imagination* ©1995, Word)

...that you may not become sluggish, but imitators of
...ose who through faith and patience inherit the
...omises. Hebrews 6:12

"More to This Life" by Steven Curtis Chapman
(*Greatest Hits* ©1997, EMD/Chordant)

...th you, Lord, everything is greater. A simple meal
... five-course dinner. A plain old field is a prairie of
...t beauty. Lord, help us to realize that all is well
...th you. Everything is stronger when you're around.
...y around us, Lord. Amen

WEEK 25

■ Psalm 78:9-16
■ Numbers 35:1-30; Luke 3:18-38

The hand of our God is gracious to all who seek him, but his power and his wrath are against all who forsake him. Ezra 8:22

> "Great Expectations" by Steven Curtis Chapman (*Speechless* ©1999, EMD/Sparrow)

Grace, mercy and peace will be with us from God the Father and from Jesus Christ, the Father's Son, in truth and love. 2 John 3

> "Glorious Grace" by Michael W. Smith (*Michael W. Smith II* ©1993, Reunion)

Heavenly Counselor, with you all is so much greater than normal. With you, a nasty rainy day is one that yields great gardens. With your love, Lord, everything has a bright side. Help us to see that bright side. Help us to know that whatever happens, you are still there by our side. Amen

WEEK 25

■ Psalm 78:17-31
■ Numbers 35:31—36:13;
Deuteronomy 1:1-18; Luke 4:1-13

I will be a wall of fire all around Jerusalem, says the LORD. Zechariah 2:5

> "Beautiful Sound" by the Newsboys (*Love Liberty Disco* ©1999, EMD/Sparrow)

Paul writes: "I am convinced that neither death, nor life, nor angels, nor rulers, nor things present, nor things to come, nor powers, nor height, nor depth, nor anything else in all creation, will be able to separate us from the love of God in Christ Jesus our Lord." Romans 8:38-39

> "Did You Feel the Mountains Tremble?" (*WoW Worship Orange* ©2000, Sony/Word)

Dearest Lord, nothing separates us from your love. Whether we like it or not, you are our Father and our protector. Protect us always, gracious Savior. Help us realize that no matter where we walk, we do not walk alone, but with you. Amen

WEEK 25

■ Psalm 78:32-39
■ Deuteronomy 1:19-46; Luke 4:14-21

e LORD, my God, lights up my darkness.
alm 18:28

| "Let Me Show You the Way" by Michael W. Smith (*Live the Life* ©1998, Reunion)

ave come as light into the world, so that everyone
o believes in me should not remain in the darkness.
n 12:46

| "Into the Light" by dc Talk (*Intermission: Greatest Hits* ©2000, EMD/Chordant)

rd, you are our light. You shine when all is dark.
d in your light, there is hope. Dearest God, we
ay that we will find that hope whenever darkness
rrounds us. Continue to be our light, Lord. May we
remember that no matter what, your light is
ning for us. Amen

WEEK 26

sunday

Watchword for the Week

Bear one another's burdens, and in
this way you fulfill the law of Christ.
Galatians 6:2

is a faithful God, without deceit, just and upright.
uteronomy 32:4

| "Let Us Pray" by Steven Curtis Chapman (*Signs of Life* ©1996, EMD/Sparrow)

we are faithless, he remains faithful—for he cannot
ny himself. 2 Timothy 2:13

| "Should've Been Loving You" by Jonathan Pierce (*Sanctuary* ©2000, Curb)

ar God, you are so loving, so caring for us, your
ldren. No matter what we do, your love is equal for
of us. Thank you, God, for always loving us equally.
ep us from wandering away from your love, Lord.
en

WEEK 26

▰▰ Psalm 78:40-55
▰▰ Deuteronomy 2:1-37; Luke 4:22-30

Those who live at earth's farthest bounds are awed by
your signs. Psalm 65:8

> "I Could Sing of Your Love Forever" by
> Sonicflood (*Sonicflood* ©1999, EMD/Chordant)

We have seen and testify that the Father has sent his
Son as the Savior of the world. 1 John 4:14

> "His Strength Is Perfect" by Steven Curtis
> Chapman (*Greatest Hits* ©1997,
> EMD/Chordant)

Father, your love shines throughout the world.
Whether it be the trees, the birds, the flowers, or the
seas, all here on earth is a testament of your love.
Thank you, Lord, for your love, may it shine on earth
for all eternity! Amen

WEEK 26

▰▰ Psalm 78:56-64
▰▰ Deuteronomy 3:1-29; Luke 4:31-44

Do not fear, O Zion; do not let your hands grow
weak. The LORD, your God, is in your midst, a warrior
who gives victory. Zephaniah 3:16-17

> "It Must Have Been Your Hands" by Clay
> Crosse (*Stained Glass* ©1997, Reunion)

Therefore lift your drooping hands and strengthen
your weak knees, and make straight paths for your
feet. Hebrews 12:12-13

> "Go There with You" by Steven Curtis
> Chapman (*Great Adventure* ©1992, Sparrow)

Jesus, it is you who keeps us strong. We pray that
you will lift us up when we fall on our walk of faith.
Son of God, all of your love shines brightly. Help us
stand firm in what we believe in, and help us do
good in your name. Amen

wednesday

Psalm 78:65-72
Deuteronomy 4:1-31; Luke 5:1-11

ll be with them in trouble, I will rescue them and
or them. Psalm 91:15

"Heavenly" by Natalie Grant (*Natalie Grant*
©1996, Provident)

s answered: "The hour is coming, indeed it has
e, when you will be scattered, each to his own
e, and you will leave me alone. Yet I am not
e because the Father is with me." John 16:32

"Wannabe Loved" by dc Talk (*Supernatural*
©1998, EMD/Virgin)

*d, we know of your love. We thank you for that
er-ending source of joy. May that joy be with us
ays, through good times, and times of trial. We
that that joy will not be hard to find, that it will
ays be there—just like you, Lord. Amen*

thursday

Psalm 79:1-8
Deuteronomy 4:32—5:21;
ke 5:12-26

o can live and never see death? Who can escape
power of Sheol? Psalm 89:48

"This Is Your Time" by Michael W. Smith (*WoW
2001* ©2000, EMD/Chordant)

raised the Lord and will also raise us by his
er. 1 Corinthians 6:14

"No You" by Zoegirl (*Zoegirl* ©2000,
EMD/Sparrow)

*ntor, heavenly Father, we know that sometimes
things happen. There is no way around this. We
however, take comfort in you. You are our
eming strength through those times of trial, and
are our beacon of light when darkness surrounds
Amen*

WEEK 26

■ Psalm 79:9-13
■ Deuteronomy 5:22—6:25;
Luke 5:27-39

Do not say, "I will do to others as they have done to me; I will pay them back for what they have done." Proverbs 24:29

"The Battle Belongs to the Lord" by Petra (*Petra Praise—Rock Cries Out* ©1989, Sony/Word)

Never avenge yourselves, but leave room for the wrath of God; for it is written, "Vengeance is mine, I will repay, says the Lord." No, "if your enemies are hungry, feed them; if they are thirsty, give them something to drink; for by doing this you will heap burning coals on their heads." Romans 12:19-20

"Speechless" by Steven Curtis Chapman (*Speechless* ©1999, EMD/Sparrow)

Gracious God, help us feel at peace even when others use or harm us. Lord, help us to remember that it is you, not us, who shall have final judgment. Help us remember that we should help all those, even our enemies, who need it. Help us fill our hearts with your love, Lord. Amen

---

WEEK 26

■ Psalm 80:1-7
■ Deuteronomy 7:1-26; Luke 6:1-11

Your days of mourning shall be ended. Isaiah 60:20

"Pray" by Rebecca St. James (*WoW 1999* ©1998, EMD/Chordant)

Paul wrote: "I consider that the sufferings of this present time are not worth comparing with the glory about to be revealed to us." Romans 8:18

"Oasis" by foreverafter (*foreverafter* ©1999, Word)

Heavenly Father, we don't know why bad things happen. We do know that you will lead us to greener pastures. Continue to guide us, faithful shepherd. Guide us to greener pastures where your light shines freely. Amen

sunday

Watchword for the Week

For by grace you have been saved through faith, and this is not your own doing; it is the gift of God. Ephesians 2:8

as for you who heap up what is not your own! How ...g will you load yourselves with goods taken in ...dge? Habakkuk 2:6

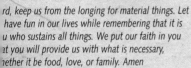

"Romans" by Jennifer Knapp (*Kansas* ©1998, EMD/Chordant)

...ep your lives free from the love of money, and be ...ntent with what you have; for he has said, "I will ...ver leave you or forsake you." Hebrews 13:5

"Fishy" by Philmore (*Philmore* ©2000, Chordant)

...rd, keep us from the longing for material things. Let ... have fun in our lives while remembering that it is ...u who sustains all things. We put our faith in you ...at you will provide us with what is necessary, ...hether it be food, love, or family. Amen

---

monday

Psalm 80:8-11
Deuteronomy 8:1—9:6; Luke 6:12-26

...en I heard the voice of the LORD saying, "Whom ...all I send, and who will go for us?" And I said: ...Here am I, send me!" Isaiah 6:8

"Find Us Faithful" by Steve Green (*Find Us Faithful* ©1988, Chordant)

...sus said: "You will receive power when the Holy ...irit has come upon you, and you will be my ...itnesses." Acts 1:8

"Spirit of the Living God" by Eden's Bridge (*Celtic Worship* ©1998, Chordant)

...oly God, you have chosen and called your people to ... your work. You send your Spirit among us for ...rength and encouragement. You give each of us ...fts to be used; yet we are often unsure of our ...ilities and ourselves. Be with us today, help us to ...ear your call, and give us the courage to respond. ...men

WEEK 27

tuesday

■ Psalm 80:12-19
■ Deuteronomy 9:7—10:22;
Luke 6:27-38

Look! On the mountains the feet of one who brings good tidings. Nahum 1:15

> "Parade" by Kathy Troccoli (*Love Has a Name* ©2000, Reunion)

Glory to God in the highest and peace on earth among those whom he favors. Luke 2:14

> "Let There Be Praise" by Sandy Patti (*Morning Like This* ©1986, Sony/Word)

Almighty God, thank you for loving us enough to become one of us. Through this act you have brought us the good news of salvation. You became our example of how to live in harmony with one another through Jesus Christ. Help us now to follow that example so that your peace may truly be felt. Amen

WEEK 27

wednesday

■ Psalm 81:1-5
■ Deuteronomy 11:1-32; Luke 6:39-49

Who can hide in secret places so that I cannot see them? says the LORD. Do I not fill heaven and earth? Jeremiah 23:24

> "Awesome God" by Rich Mullins (*Songs* ©1996, Reunion)

See, I am with you always, to the end of the age. Matthew 28:20

> "I've Always Loved You" by Third Day (*Time* ©1999, BMG/Jive/Silvertone)

Ever-present Lord, there are many times in our lives when we run from you. We like the illusion that we are in control. Yet in the toughest times, though we may not feel your presence, you are there. Your love never leaves us. Please continue to be with us today and for the rest of our lives. Amen

Psalm 81:6-10
Deuteronomy 12:1-32; Luke 7:1-17

e in me, a clean heart, O God, and give me a right spirit. Psalm 51:10

"Surrender" by Glenn Kaiser (*All My Days* ©Grrr Records. For more information, click on www.glennkaiser.com)

vell that the heart be strengthened by grace. ews 13:9

"Amazing Grace" by Terry McMillan (*Somebody's Comin'* ©1997, WEA/Warner Brothers)

re our refuge and strength, O God. Through t's sacrifice and victory over death we have been . Through your great grace we can bring our sins u and know they are forgiven. Help us to always mber this gift so we may be strengthened by it.

Psalm 81:11-16
Deuteronomy 13:1—14:21;
e 7:18-30

stone which the builders rejected has become hief cornerstone. That is the LORD's doing; and it rvelous in our eyes. Psalm 118:22-23

"Mighty Is Our God" (*WoW Worship: Today's 30 Most Powerful Worship Songs* ©1999, Sony/Word)

en you are no longer strangers and aliens, you tizens with the saints and also members of the ehold of God, built on the foundation of the les and prophets, with Jesus Christ as the rstone. Ephesians 2:19-20

"Circle of Friends" by Point of Grace (*Live Love & Other Mysteries* ©1996, Sony/Word)

t Jesus, you are our strength and our salvation. lone have become the cornerstone of our lives. gh your loving sacrifice we become family. k you for all you have done. Please continue to us the strength to do your will. Be our corner- of faith now and always. Amen

WEEK 27

■ Psalm 82:1-4
■ Deuteronomy 14:22—15:18;
Luke 7:31-39

Your servant is warned through your commandments.
Psalm 19:11

"Basic Instructions" by Burlap to Cashmere
(*Anybody Out There?* ©1998 UNI/Eureka/ILS)

Jesus said: "I am the way and the truth and the life,
no one comes to the Father except through me."
John 14:6

"Lord of the Dance" by Steven Curtis Chapman
(*Signs of Life* ©1996, EMD/Sparrow)

*Lord Jesus, you indeed are the way to God. You have
shown the love of God and neighbor to us, and ask
us to follow that example. Continue to guide us in
your ways, helping us to know and follow your commands so that we too might come into the Father's
presence. Amen*

WEEK 28

Watchword for the Week
Do not fear, for I have redeemed
you; I have called you by name, you
are mine. Isaiah 43:1

Now begin the work, and the LORD be with you.
1 Chronicles 22:16

"I'll Be" by Reba McEntire (*So Good Together*
©1999, UNI/MCA Nashville)

Cast all your anxieties on him, because he cares for
you. 1 Peter 5:7

"Thankful" by Caedmon's Call (*40 Acres* ©1999,
BMG/Brentwood)

*Caring Lord, you are always with us in all we do. We
can bring to you all our problems. Even though we
know this, we do not always feel your presence. As we
go about our day, Lord, help us to be aware of your
loving presence and the peace that it brings. Amen*

Psalm 82:5-8
Deuteronomy 15:19—17:7;
...ke 7:40-50

...shall rise before the aged, and defer to the old.
...ticus 19:32

"Prayer Warrior" by Heirloom (*Twenty Number One Christian Hits* ©1994, Reunion)

...dren, obey your parents in the Lord, for this is ...t. And fathers, do not provoke your children to ...er, but bring them up in the discipline and instruc-...n of the Lord. Ephesians 6:1, 4

"As It Is in Heaven" by Michael W. Smith (*I'll Lead You Home* ©1995 Reunion)

...heavenly Father, through the wisdom of our ...ers you have given us a source of knowledge and ...erstanding. You have asked that we listen so we ...y learn more fully how to obey you and do your ...t. Give us ears to hear and the insight to follow ...r will. Amen

Psalm 83:1-8
Deuteronomy 17:8—18:22;
...ke 8:1-15

...ar, O Israel, the LORD is our God, the LORD alone.
...uteronomy 6:4

"Blessed Be the Lord God Almighty" (*WoW Worship: Today's 30 Most Powerful Worship Songs* ©1999, Sony/Word)

...l said: "For as I went through the city and looked ...efully at the objects of your worship, I found ...ong them an altar with the inscription, 'To an ...nown god.' What therefore you worship as ...nown, this I proclaim to you." Acts 17:22-23

"I Want to Know You (In the Secret)" by Sonicflood (*WoW 2000,* ©1999, EMD/Chordant)

...r only true God, thank you for your powerful ...sence in our lives. Through Christ we have come ...know you and call you our Lord, our Father. Help ...to spread your love and help others to know you ...we know you. Amen

WEEK 28

■ **Psalm 83:9-12**
■ **Deuteronomy 19:1—20:9;**
Luke 8:16-25

The LORD has sent me to provide for those who mourn in Zion, to give them a garland instead of ashes, the oil of gladness instead of mourning, the mantle of praise instead of a faint spirit. Isaiah 61:2-3

> "Praise Adonai" by Paul Baloche (*Open the Eyes of My Heart* ©2000, Integrity)

Blessed are those who mourn, for they shall be comforted. Matthew 5:4

> "Get Down" by Audio Adrenaline (*WoW 2000*, ©1999, EMD/Chordant)

Grieving God, you are with us even in our sorrow. You seek to comfort us in a time when it feels as if no comfort will ever help. Let us know your peace in the midst of chaos and trial. Let us know the comfort of you in our lives. Amen

WEEK 28

■ **Psalm 83:13-18**
■ **Deuteronomy 20:10—21:21;**
Luke 8:26-39

For you have delivered my soul from death, and my feet from falling, so that I may walk before God in the light of life. Psalm 56:13

> "Flood" by Jars of Clay (*Jars of Clay* ©1995, BMG/Jive/Silvertone)

The man answered: "The man called Jesus made mud, spread it on my eyes, and said: 'Go to Siloam and wash.' Then I went and washed and received my sight." John 9:11

> "Great Is the Lord" by Michael W. Smith (*First Decade—1983-93* ©1993, Reunion)

Precious Jesus, while you walked on earth you performed great miracles that showed the power given to you by God. As you helped those you were with so long ago, help us today. Deliver us, lift us up, open our eyes, and give us understanding that we may live a life pleasing to you. Amen

friday

Psalm 84:1-7
Deuteronomy 21:22—22:30;
Luke 8:40-56

The LORD has granted the petition which I made to him. 1 Samuel 1:27

"Give Thanks" by Don Moen (*Songs for Worship: Shout to the Lord* ©2001, WEA/ Time-Life)

The angel said to him, "Do not be afraid, Zechariah, for your prayer has been heard. Your wife Elizabeth will bear you a son, and you will name him John." Luke 1:13

"More Love, More Power" (*WoW Worship: Today's 30 Most Powerful Worship Songs* ©1999, Sony/Word)

Listening Lord, you have heard the prayers of your people since the beginning. You have answered those prayers according to your will. Lord, hear our prayers now, listen to our yearnings, and know our minds and hearts, yet in all things let your will be done. Amen

---

saturday

Psalm 84:8-12
Deuteronomy 23:1—24:13;
Luke 9:1-11

Our God turned the curse into a blessing. Nehemiah 13:2

"Change My Heart, Oh God" (*America's 25 Favorite Acoustic Worship 1* ©1998, Provident)

Do not repay evil for evil or abuse for abuse, on the contrary repay with a blessing. 1 Peter 3:9

"Let It Go" by the Newsboys (*Take Me to Your Leader* ©1996, EMD/Chordant)

Awesome God, you are able to make a blessing out of the worst situations. You have given us an example of how to show love and kindness in the midst of adversity through the ministry of Christ. Help us to fight the urge to retaliate, and instead show your love. Amen

WEEK 29

Watchword for the Week
So you are no longer strangers and aliens, but you are citizens with the saints and members of God's household. Ephesians 2:19

I rise before dawn and cry for help; I put my hope in your words. Psalm 119:147

"Trading My Sorrows" (*WoW Green* ©2001, Sony/Epic)

Jesus spoke to the official, "Go, your son will live." The man believed the word that Jesus spoke to him and started on his way. John 4:50

"Rise up and Praise Him" (*WoW Green* ©2001, Sony/Epic)

Most holy Lord God, you have willingly taken our sins. But just as we give you the biggest problems and concerns in our lives, help us to remember that you care about the littlest things as well. Help us to completely lay down our sorrows, sickness, and grief at your feet and in exchange pick up your joy, blessings, and power. Amen

WEEK 29

▬ Psalm 85:1-7
▬ Deuteronomy 24:14—25:19;
Luke 9:12-27

I will meditate on all your work, and muse on your mighty deeds. Psalm 77:12

"Change My Heart, Oh God" (*WoW Worship: Today's 30 Most Powerful Worship Songs* ©1999, Sony/Word)

Mary Magdalene went and announced to the disciples: "I have seen the Lord"; and she told them that he had said these things to her. John 20:18

"Easter Song" by Second Chapter of Acts (*WoW Gold* ©2000, BMG/Brentwood)

Resurrected Lord, remind us of the miracle Mary Magdalene witnessed. We too have seen your presence in our lives. Give us the words as well as the courage to speak these words to those in our circle of friends. May we be a testimony to your power to change our lives and your faithfulness to complete your work. Amen

tuesday

Psalm 85:8-12
Deuteronomy 26:1—27:13;
e 9:28-36

e put my words in your mouth and hidden you in
hadow of my hand. Isaiah 51:16

"Lord, I Lift Your Name on High" by Petra
(*Petra Praise 2: We Need Jesus* ©1997,
Sony/Word)

laid his hands on the afflicted woman; and
diately she rose up and praised God. Luke 13:13

"More Than Wonderful" by Sandi Patti and
Larnelle Harris (*More Than Wonderful* ©1990,
Word)

us, Lord, to always remember to praise you.
situations are difficult and all hope seems lost,
d us that you are the way; that you light our
Let us focus our thoughts on your faithfulness,
we might reflect your love just as a lantern
ts light in the darkness. Amen

wednesday

Psalm 86:1-10
Deuteronomy 27:14—28:24;
e 9:37-50

spoke to Moses: I Am Who I Am. Exodus 3:14

"Awesome God" by Rich Mullins (*WoW Gold*
©2000, BMG/Brentwood)

the Alpha and the Omega," says God the Lord,
ho was and is and is to come, the Almighty.
lation 1:8

"God" by Rebecca St. James (*WoW Gold*
©2000, BMG/Brentwood)

we cannot begin to comprehend your presence.
in our hearts and minds. Help us experience
love and power in direct ways. Please keep our
from trying to make you small. We know you
ot some man behind a curtain—like in the
rd of Oz—but sometimes we treat you that way.
e forgive us. Amen

WEEK 29

■ Psalm 86:11-17
■ Deuteronomy 28:25-57; Luke 9:51-62

Then shall the eyes of the blind be opened and the ears of the deaf unstopped. Isaiah 35:5

> "The Reason We Sing" by First Call (*Somethin' Takes Over* ©1987, Word)

We are God's children now; what we will be has not yet been revealed. What we do know is that when he is revealed, we will be like him, for we will see him as he is. 1 John 3:2

> "The Now and the Not Yet" by Amy Grant (*Straight Ahead* ©1984, Myrrh)

Lord, we could really use some answers. Why are our problems so overwhelming? Where are you in the pain and suffering? Where are you in life's injustices? Teach us your ways and give us patience and understanding so we can recognize that we are only seeing part of your plan. Help us to trust you. Amen

WEEK 29

■ Psalm 87
■ Deuteronomy 28:58—29:21; Luke 10:1-16

For the LORD is a God of justice; blessed are all those who wait for him. Isaiah 30:18

> "The Sheep and the Goats" by Keith Green (*Songs of Evangelism* ©1998, Chordant)

For by grace you have been saved by faith, and this is not your own doing; it is the gift of God. Ephesians 2:8

> "The Gift Goes On" by Sandi Patti (*The Gift Goes On* ©1987, Word)

O God, your grace is so far beyond our understanding that we can scarcely take it in. Thank you for this wonderful gift! Give us the desire to share your gift with others. Teach us that the gift of your love becomes even more complete in our lives when we share it with others. Amen

WEEK 29

saturday

Psalm 88:1-5

Deuteronomy 29:22—31:6;
Luke 10:17-24

You shall not covet your neighbor's wife.
Deuteronomy 5:21

"Busy Man" by Steven Curtis Chapman *(For the Sake of the Call* ©1990, Sparrow)

Love does no wrong to a neighbor. Romans 13:10

"Undivided" by First Call *(Undivided* ©1986, Word)

Forgive us for wanting that which belongs to our friends. Help us to learn contentment. Remind us that the toys of this life are simply that—toys—and that only in you will we find things of lasting value. Help us to take time for the people in our lives. Keep us from being too busy to love others. Amen

WEEK 30

sunday

Watchword for the Week

Live as children of the light: for the fruit of the light is found in all that is good and right and true.
Ephesians 5:8-9

I have been with you wherever you went. 2 Samuel 7:9

"I Am the Way" by Mark Schultz *(Mark Schultz* ©2000, Sony/Word)

Jesus Christ says: "Abide in me and I in you."
John 15:4

"My Will" by dc Talk *(Intermission: Greatest Hits* ©2000, EMD/Chordant)

Your will has become ours, O heavenly Father. Wherever we go, we know you are always there. Through all the joys and even sorrows of our lives, you are standing forever with us. Amen

WEEK 30

monday

■ Psalm 88:6-12
■ Deuteronomy 31:7—32:8;
Luke 10:25-42

My times are in your hand. Psalm 31:15

"Take Me In" by Petra (*Petra Praise: Rock Cries Out* ©1989, Sony/Word)

Because I live, you also will live. John 14:19

"Can't Live a Day" by Avalon (*In a Different Light* ©1999, EMD/Sparrow)

Please guide us by your footsteps, Lord. Remind us each day that we only live because of your great sacrifice for us. Without you, we face no morning or night, and we breathe because you have breathed. Amen

WEEK 30

tuesday

■ Psalm 88:13-18
■ Deuteronomy 32:9-43; Luke 11:1-13

I, the LORD, am your Savior and your Redeemer, the Mighty One. Isaiah 60:16

"Awesome God" by Rich Mullins (*Songs 4 Life: Feel the Power* ©1998, WEA/Time-Life)

They said to the woman: "It is no longer because of what you said that we believe; for we have heard for ourselves; and we know that this is truly the Savior of the world." John 4:42

"Face of Love" by Jewel (*Joy: Holiday Collection* ©1999, WEA/Atlantic))

Lord God, you reign from your mighty kingdom on heaven and earth to show us every day—whether it be at school, at work, or at leisure—that you truly are an awesome God. We have seen for ourselves that you are almighty and powerful. Amen

WEEK 30

Psalm 89:1-8
Deuteronomy 32:44—33:21;
Luke 11:14-28

The LORD said to Moses: "Who gives speech to mortals? Is it not I, the LORD? Now go, and I will be with your mouth and teach you what you are to speak." Exodus 4:11-12

"When You Called My Name" by the Newsboys (*Going Public* ©1994, EMD/Sparrow)

Those who speak on their own seek their own glory; but the one who seeks the glory of him who sent him is true, and there is nothing false in him. John 7:18

"Speak to Me" by Rebecca St. James (*God* ©1996, EMD/Chordant)

When you called us by name, we did not understand. Now we stand as your children before you. Unveil our senses and speak to us. Let us know that you are the true and one living Lord. Amen

WEEK 30

Psalm 89:9-18
Deuteronomy 33:22—34:12;
Joshua 1:1-18; Luke 11:29-36

Is it not you, O LORD our God? We set our hope on you. Jeremiah 14:22

"Smell the Color Nine" by Chris Rice (*Smell the Color Nine* ©2000, Sony/Word)

So neither the one who plants nor the one who waters is anything, but only God who gives the growth. 1 Corinthians 3:7

"God Is in Control" by Twila Paris (*Songs 4 Life: Feel the Power* ©1998, WEA/Time-Life)

You are the living water, ever-flowing with the unconditional love that enables us to grow. Our hope and faith are in you and only you, now and forever; even if at times we find it hard to see or hear you, we know you are with us. Amen

WEEK 30

■ Psalm 89:19-29
■ Joshua 2:1-24; Luke 11:37-54

Return, O faithless children, I will heal your faithlessness. Jeremiah 3:22

> "Heart of a Champion" by Carman (*Heart of a
> Champion* ©2000, EMD/Sparrow)

For God has imprisoned all in disobedience so that he
may be merciful to all. Romans 11:32

> "Humble Thyself in the Sight of the Lord" by
> Luna Halo (*Listen: Louder* ©1999, Chordant)

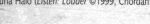

*Lord Jesus, we pray to have faith in all that we do.
You have seen us as children, misguided, restore our
faith in you. Keep us humble so we realize everything
we do is for you, not ourselves, and be merciful when
we fail to do your will. Amen*

WEEK 30

■ Psalm 89:30-37
■ Joshua 3:1—4:24; Luke 12:1-12

Sing to the LORD; praise the LORD! For he has delivered the life of the needy from the hands of evildoers.
Jeremiah 20:13

> "He Is Exalted" by Twila Paris (*Songs 4
> Worship: Shout to the Lord* ©2001 WEA/
> Time-Life)

Are any among you suffering? They should pray. Are
any cheerful? They should sing songs of praise.
James 5:13

> "Just a Prayer Away" by Jaci Velasquez (*Crystal
> Clear* ©2000, Sony/Word)

*Through any troubles we may have throughout our
day, almighty God, we know you are always here for
us. We praise and thank you, precious Jesus, for
everything you have brought to our lives. Amen*

sunday

Watchword for the Week
From everyone to whom much has been given, much will be required; and from the one to whom much has been entrusted, even more will be demanded. Luke 12:48

...opy are those who consider the poor. The LORD ...vers them in the day of trouble. Psalm 41:1

"Revive Us" by Anointed (*Anointed* ©1999, Sony/Word)

...anyone among you who is without sin be the first ...throw a stone at her. John 8:7

"Broken" by The Altar Boys (*Gut Level Music/Against the Grain* ©1998, Provident)

...ase, Lord, help us to be kind to the needy and not ...ass judgment. For we know that one day you will ...ge us as we have judged others. We ask for forgive-...s for times we failed to be like you. Amen

monday

Psalm 89:38-45
Joshua 5:1—6:27; Luke 12:13-21

...en to me, my people, and give heed to me, my ...on; for a teaching will go out from me, and my ...ce for a light to the peoples. Isaiah 51:4

"Seek Ye First" by The Marantha Singers (*Songs 4 Worship: Holy Ground* ©2001, WEA/ Time-Life)

...did not send his Son into the world to condemn ...world, but in order that the world might be saved ...ugh him. John 3:17

"You Breathe" by Nouveaux (*And This Is How I Feel* ©1996, Benson)

...oly Father, please give us the ears to hear your ...ds so that your will may be done. Teach us your ...s, for you have given us life, and saved our lives ...acrificing yours. Amen

WEEK 31

▬▬ Psalm 89:46-52
▬▬ Joshua 7:1-26; Luke 12:22-34

I proclaimed a fast that we might deny ourselves before our God, to seek from him a safe journey. Ezra 8:21

| "Just a Closer Walk with Thee" by Bobby Jones/Maya Angelou (*M2K Gospel 2000* ©2000, UNI/Gospocentric)

They saw Jesus walking on the sea near the boat, and they were terrified. But he said to them, "It is I, be not afraid." John 6:19-20

| "Love Song" by Third Day (*Offerings: A Worship Album* ©2000, BMG/Brentwood)

O merciful Savior, we pray to die to self so that we will be more like you and your sacrifices for us. Grant us discernment so that we are not fearful of the glorious miracles you accomplish every day. Amen

WEEK 31

▬▬ Psalm 90
▬▬ Joshua 8:1-29; Luke 12:35-53

O come, let us worship and bow down, let us kneel before the LORD our Maker. Psalm 95:6

| "God You Are My God" by Delirious? (*Glo* ©2000, EMD/Sparrow)

Be renewed in the spirit of your minds and clothe yourselves with the new self, created according to the likeness of God in true righteousness and holiness. Ephesians 4:23-24

| "Holiness" by Sonicflood (*Sonicflood* ©1999, EMD/Chordant)

We come before you, almighty King of glory, so that you may purify our hearts, transform our wills, and cleanse our souls. We ask that you renew our spirits so that we are truly able to handle whatever this day may bring. Amen

WEEK 31

thursday

Psalm 91:1-8
Joshua 8:30—9:27; Luke 12:54—13:5

u, O Lᴏʀᴅ, are our father; our Redeemer from of
d is your name. Isaiah 63:16

"Blessed Be the Name of the Lord" (*Songs for
Worship: Be Glorified* ©2001, WEA/Time-Life)

sus Christ said: "My Father is still working, and I
o am working." John 5:17

"Father, I Adore You" (*WoW Worship—Today's
30 Most Powerful Worship Songs* ©1999,
Sony/Word)

ar heavenly Father, our first and perfect parent,
u are with us. Your power and presence surround
 yet we sometimes fail to see you. Help us, Lord, to
d you and recognize your work in the actions of
ends, in the faces of strangers, and in your glorious
ated world. This we pray in Jesus' name. Amen

WEEK 31

friday

Psalm 91:9-16
Joshua 10:1-28; Luke 13:6-17

no am I, and what is my people, that we should be
e to make this freewill offering? For all things come
m you, and of your own have we given you.
Chronicles 29:14

"Give Thanks" (*Australia's Top 25 Praise Songs*
©2001, Maranatha!)

d is able to provide you with every blessing in
undance, so that by always having enough of
erything, you may share abundantly in every good
rk. 2 Corinthians 9:8

"Three Little Birds" by Bob Marley (*Exodus*
©1977, Island)

nevolent God, we thank you for the many bless-
s in our lives as well as life itself. With all of its
s and all of its heartaches, life is always our most
ecious gift. Help us to see your blessings all around
 Amen

WEEK 31

■ Psalm 92:1-8
■ Joshua 10:29—11:23; Luke 13:18-30

In your hand are power and might; and it is in your hand to make great and to give strength to all.
1 Chronicles 29:12

> "Come and Take My Hand" by Out of Eden, (*Lovin' the Day* ©1994, EMI/Chordant)

Peter spoke to the people in the temple: "The faith that is through Jesus, has given him this perfect health in the presence of all of you." Acts 3:12, 16

> "More Love, More Power" (*Vol. 1—Change My Heart Oh God* ©1996, EMD/Chordant)

God of strength, God of renewal, pour your power onto us this day. Revive our tired spirits and bodies. Strengthen us for doing your work in the world. Open our minds to new possibilities; show us new ways of being your faithful people. In our Savior's name we pray. Amen

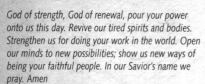

WEEK 32

Watchword for the Week
Happy is the nation whose God is the LORD, the people whom he has chosen as his heritage. Psalm 33:12

I will again do amazing things with this people, shocking and amazing. The wisdom of their wise shall perish. Isaiah 29:14

> "Almighty" by Wayne Watson (*Wayne Watson: Very Best* ©1995, Word)

Jesus Christ said to the Samaritan woman: "You worship what you do not know, we worship what we know; for salvation is from the Jews." John 4:22

> "El Shaddai" by Michael Card (*Joy in the Journey* ©1994, EMD/Sparrow)

God of wisdom, we ask you to guide us into the truth. Enable us to discern your divine wisdom from human wisdom. Give us grace this day and always to gently lead others to your fellowship so that they too may live in the knowledge of your love and grace. This we pray in Jesus' name. Amen

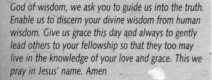

WEEK 32

Psalm 92:9-15

Joshua 12:1—13:7; Luke 13:31—14:6

The LORD before whom I walk will send his angel with you and make your way successful. Genesis 24:40

"Thy Word" (*Word Gold—Five Decades of Hits* ©2001, Sony/Word)

During the night Paul had a vision; there stood a man from Macedonia pleading with him: "Come over, and help us." When he had seen the vision, we immediately tried to cross over to Macedonia, being convinced that God had called us to proclaim the good news to them. Acts 16:9-10

"Shine Jesus, Shine" (*Australia's Top 25 Praise Songs* ©2001, Maranatha!)

Lord, your love surrounds us wherever we go. Help us to recognize your loving presence in our lives. Light our path today so that we may go in your peace and love. Amen

---

WEEK 32

Psalm 93

Joshua 13:8—14:5; Luke 14:7-24

Praise God in the assembly. Psalm 68:26

"He Is Exalted" (*Australia's Top 25 Praise Songs* ©2001, Maranatha!)

Encourage one another as you sing psalms and hymns and spiritual songs among yourselves, singing and making melody to the Lord in your hearts, giving thanks to God the Father at all times and for everything in the name of our Lord Jesus Christ. Ephesians 5:19-20

"Shout to the Lord" (*Australia's Top 25 Praise Songs* ©2001, Maranatha!)

Gracious God, it is amazing that in praising you we find ourselves blessed. You hear our prayers and our songs and, finding pleasure in them, bless us in return. We are grateful for your many blessings and for the strength we receive from you. Empower us this day, Lord, to do your work; at home, at school, at work. Amen

WEEK 32

■ Psalm 94:1-11
■ Joshua 14:6—15:19; Luke 14:25-35

Obey my voice and I will be your God, and you shall be my people. Jeremiah 7:23

> "Love of My Life" by Carlos Santana (*Supernatural* ©1999, Arista)

Try to find out what is pleasing to the Lord. Ephesians 5:10

> "Christafari" by Christafari (*Soulfire* ©1994. For more information, click on www.christafari.com)

Lord, open our hearts to the sound of your voice. We know you are calling. Enable us to truly hear you. We want to follow you in all aspects of life. Give us the strength to do so. May we walk in the light of your love, today and always. Amen

WEEK 32

■ Psalm 94:12-23
■ Joshua 15:20-60; Luke 15:1-10

God looks to the ends of the earth, and sees everything under the heavens. Job 28:24

> "Great Is the Lord" by Michael W. Smith (*First Decade 1983-93* ©1993, Reunion)

Now I know partially; but then I shall know fully as I have been known. 1 Corinthians 13:12

> "Just As I Am" by Deniece Williams (*This Is My Song* ©1998, Harmony)

Lord, you know us completely, our strengths, our weaknesses, everything. There is nothing we can hide from you. Yet, knowing everything about us, you still love us. We are grateful for your never-ending love. We celebrate this blessing and in return will share it with others. In Jesus' name we pray. Amen

thursday

friday

■ Psalm 95
Joshua 15:61—17:18; Luke 15:11-32

t one word has failed of all his good promise,
ch he spoke through his servant Moses.
ings 8:56

"My Life Is in You, Lord" (*WoW Worship—
Today's 30 Most Powerful Worship Songs*
©1999, Sony/Word)

whom God has sent, speaks the word of God; for
gives the Spirit without measure. John 3:34

"Spirit of the Living God" by Any Given Day
(*Passionate Worship for the Soul* ©2001,
EMD/Chordant)

y Spirit, we ask you to blow your winds of
ewal and power into our lives and the lives of
se around us. Blow away all hatred and prejudice;
g your love and compassion. This we pray in
us' name. Amen

saturday

■ Psalm 96:1-9
■ Joshua 18:1—19:9; Luke 16:1-15

do not present our supplication before you on the
und of our righteousness, but on the ground of
r great mercies. Daniel 9:18

"I Can't Keep Goin' On and On" by Take 6
(*Join the Band* ©1994, WEA/Warner Brothers)

sed be the God and Father of our Lord Jesus
ist! By his great mercy he has given us a new birth
a living hope through the resurrection of Jesus
ist from the dead. 1 Peter 1:3

"Lord, I Lift Your Name on High" by Lincoln
Brewster (*Live to Worship* ©2000, Sony/Word)

, you are the source of our strength. Empower us
erve you through our bodies, minds, and hearts.
we be strong for you. Amen

WEEK 33

Watchword for the Week
God opposes the proud, but gives grace to the humble. 1 Peter 5:5

Do not be afraid or dismayed; for the LORD God, my God, is with you. He will not fail you nor forsake you, until all the work for the service of the house of the LORD is finished. 1 Chronicles 28:20

| "True North" by Twila Paris (*True North*, ©1999, EMD/Sparrow)

Jesus said to the disciples: "Cast the net on the right side of the boat, and you will find some." So they cast it, and now they were not able to haul it in because there were so many fish. John 21:6

| "Step by Step" by Rich Mullins (*Vol. 1—World As Best As I Remember It* ©1991, Reunion)

Lord, we stand tall because we know you are leading us. You are our strength and our redeemer; we find peace and joy in you. Help us to stay strong even when we are ridiculed for our faith. Amen

WEEK 33

■ **Psalm 96:10-13**
■ **Joshua 19:10-38; Luke 16:16-31**

Your eyes are open to all the ways of mortals. Jeremiah 32:19

| "Take My Life" (*America's 25 Favorite Hymns 3* ©1997, BMG/Brentwood)

Jesus Christ said: "I am not asking you to take them out of the world, but I ask you to protect them from the evil one." John 17:15

| "Imagine" by John Lennon (*Imagine* ©1971, EMD/Capitol)

Glorious God, we long for a perfect world. We live in a broken world where greed and hatred seem to be everywhere. Yet, even in the darkest places you are there, working through those who know your love. We thank you Lord, for not giving up on us. Work within us today. Amen

tuesday

Psalm 97:1-6
Joshua 19:39—21:8; Luke 17:1-5

The LORD opens the eyes of the blind. Psalm 146:8

"Open Our Eyes, Lord" (*Acoustic Worship 1* ©1998, BMG/Brentwood)

Let everyone who is thirsty come. Let anyone who wishes take the water as a gift. Revelation 22:17

"Let the River Flow" (*WoW Worship—Today's 30 Most Powerful Worship Songs* ©1999, Sony/Word)

Loving God, we are so fortunate to live in your love and fellowship. Enable us to welcome new people into our community of faith with the same love that you extend to us. Walk with us wherever we go sharing your peace and grace. Amen

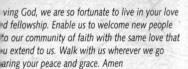

---

wednesday

Psalm 97:7-12
Joshua 21:9-45; Luke 17:6-19

Great is our LORD, and abundant in power. Psalm 147:5

"Great Is the Lord" by Michael W. Smith (*First Decade 1983-93* ©1993, Reunion)

Martha spoke to Jesus: "Lord, if you had been here, my brother would not have died. But even now I know that God will give you whatever you ask of him." John 11:21-22

"One Single Light" by Phillips, Craig, and Dean (*Restoration* ©1999, EMD/Sparrow)

Lord, help us to have faith even when we feel like Martha. Remind us when we feel your timing is not our timing that you are never too late; that you are always in control. In our hearts we know you are trustworthy. Let us lift our voices to you in praise. Amen

WEEK 33

■ Psalm 98
■ Joshua 22:1-34; Luke 17:20-25

Seek the LORD and his strength, seek his presence continually. Psalm 105:4

> "Seek Ye First" (*Vol. 2—Acoustic Worship* ©1999, BMG/Brentwood)

From one ancestor he made all nations to inhabit the earth, and he allotted the times of their existence and the boundaries of the places where they would live. Acts 17:26

> "Ancient of Days" (*WoW Worship—Today's 30 Most Powerful Worship Songs* ©1999, Sony/Word)

Lord, we seek your order in our lives. Enable us to prioritize the competing needs of family, church, school, and social activities. Help us find your balance in all things. Amen

WEEK 33

■ Psalm 99
■ Joshua 23:1—24:13; Luke 17:26-37

You shepherds, you have been feeding yourselves. Should not shepherds feed the sheep? Ezekiel 34:2

> "More Than Enough" by the Brooklyn Tabernacle Choir (*God Is Working—Live* ©2000, Sony/Word)

The hired hand, who is not the shepherd, and does not own the sheep, sees the wolf coming and leaves the sheep and runs away. I am the good shepherd. I know my own and my own know me. John 10:12, 14

> "Shepherd of My Heart" by Sandi Patti (*Morning Like This* ©1986, Sony/Word)

Jesus, thank you for your faithfulness to us, as a shepherd cares for his sheep. Surely you will meet our every need, and give out of your bounty. Lord, we offer up to you our requests, burdens, desires, and dreams, because you care for us. Amen

WEEK 33

Psalm 100

Joshua 24:14-33; Judges 1:1-6;
...ke 18:1-17

...ave no dread or fear. The LORD your God, who goes
...fore you, is the one who will fight for you.
...euteronomy 1:29-30

"Did You Feel the Mountains Tremble?" by
Delirious? (*Cutting Edge* ©1997, EMD/Sparrow)

...sus Christ said: "In the world you face persecution.
...t take courage; I have conquered the world."
...nn 16:33

"Lifeboat" by the Elms (*Big Surprise* ©2001,
EMD/Chordant)

...ghty God, there is no other power on heaven or on
...rth that can shake mountains, and we will put our
...pe in you. Praise be to you because of the victory
...t Jesus has over sin and death. Thank you that
...ur victory, Jesus, is real and can be appropriated in
...r lives. Amen

WEEK 34

Watchword for the Week
A bruised reed he will not break,
and a dimly burning wick he will not
quench. Isaiah 42:3

...cause the LORD is at my right hand, I shall not be
...ved. Psalm 16:8

"Shaken Up" by Delirious? (*Cutting Edge* ©1997,
EMD/Sparrow)

...th all of these, take the shield of faith, with which
...u will be able to quench all the flaming arrows of the
...l one. Ephesians 6:16

"A Shield about Me" (*Nitro Praise 5* ©Diamante)

...us, so often our lives feel shaken up and unground-
...Lord, we want to know the security of your hand
...r our lives, and the power of the shield of faith,
...ch helps us to fight off the enemy's arrows. Amen

WEEK 34

▬ Psalm 101
▬ Judges 1:17—2:23; Luke 18:18-30

When all the enemies heard of it, they were afraid; for they perceived that this work had been accomplished with the help of our God. Nehemiah 6:16

> "When the Righteous Prosper" (*Rejoice Africa* ©Hosanna! For more information click on www.integritymusic.com)

The jailer called for lights, and fell trembling before Paul and Silas. Then he brought them outside and said: "Sirs, what must I do to be saved?" They answered: "Believe on the Lord Jesus, and you will be saved, you and your household." Acts 16:29-31

> "We Cry Holy" (*Rejoice Africa* ©Hosanna! For more information click on www.integritymusic.com)

Holy One, who wouldn't fall down trembling in your presence? Your holiness, the very thing that sets you apart, is the very thing that we need in our lives. We shout for joy because even our enemies fear you! Amen

WEEK 34

▬ Psalm 102:1-11
▬ Judges 3:1-31; Luke 18:31-43

The heavens are yours, the earth also is yours; you have founded them. The north and the south—you created them. Psalm 89:11-12

> "Your Love, Oh Lord" by Third Day (*Offerings: A Worship Album* ©2000, BMG/Brentwood)

All things hold together in [Christ]. He is the head of the body, the church. Colossians 1:17-18

> "Superman" by Luna Halo (*Shimmer* ©2000, EMD/Sparrow)

Creator God, we give you all the glory for creating the heavens and the earth. We submit our lives to your lordship, Christ, because you have earned that position by your death and resurrection. Teach us to respect authority. Amen

WEEK 34

Psalm 102:12-22

Judges 4:1-24; Luke 19:1-10

You have made my days a few handbreadths, and my lifetime is as nothing in your sight. Surely everyone stands as a mere breath. Psalm 39:5

> "Breathe" (*Word Gold: Five Decades of Hits* ©2001, Sony/Word)

Jesus Christ said: "This is indeed the will of my Father, that all who see the Son and believe in him may have eternal life." John 6:40

> "My Glorious" by Delirious? (*Glo* ©2000, EMD/Sparrow)

Holy Spirit, you are the air we breathe, and our life doesn't amount to much without you, Jesus. You have taken our old life and given us something new. Now we have a greater purpose: to serve the king and help build the kingdom! Thank you for allowing us to be part of your work, Lord. Amen

---

WEEK 34

Psalm 102:23-28

Judges 5:1-31; Luke 19:11-27

So those in the west shall fear the name of the LORD and those in the east, his glory. Isaiah 59:19

> "Shout to the North" by Delirious? (*Cutting Edge* ©1997, EMD/Sparrow)

And he has put all things under his feet and has made him the head over all things for his body the church. Ephesians 1:22

> "You Alone" by Lincoln Brewster (*Live to Worship* ©2000, Sony/Word)

Jesus, as we call you Lord, we are freed to dance and sing before you. Thank you that you are Lord of the east and the west, and that we can have you in common with someone across the world! God, we pray that you would use us to shout out your name across the earth. Amen

WEEK 34

▪▪▪ Psalm 103:1-5
▪▪▪ Judges 6:1-40; Luke 19:28-44

Fear God, and keep his commandments, for that is the whole duty of everyone. Ecclesiastes 12:13

> "Hands and Feet" by Audio Adrenaline (*Hit Parade* ©2001, EMD/Chordant)

By this we know that we love the children of God, when we love God and keep his commandments. 1 John 5:2

> "Hope to Carry On" by Caedmon's Call (*1998 Dove Award Nominees: Best In Christian Music* ©1998, BMG/Brentwood)

Lord, thank you for giving us rules to play by. Without them we would be lost in life. God, we pray that you would help us live by your commandments so we can enjoy the perfection of your will for our lives. Amen

WEEK 34

▪▪▪ Psalm 103:6-18
▪▪▪ Judges 7:1-25; Luke 19:45—20:8

You are God, you alone, of all the kingdoms of the earth; you have made heaven and earth. 2 Kings 19:15

> "God of Wonders" by Mac Powell and Cliff Danielle Young (*City on a Hill* ©2000, BMG/Jive/Silvertone)

To the king of the ages, immortal, invisible, the only God, be honor and glory forever and ever. Amen 1 Timothy 1:17

> "Glorify Thy Name" (*America's 25 Favorite Acoustic Worship 4* ©2000, BMG/Brentwood)

God, your wonders cause us to glorify your name! We pray that every area of our lives would be glorifying to you. God, show us creative ways so that we can express our worship to you, our king! Amen

WEEK 35

sunday

Watchword for the Week

Christ says: "What you have done to the least of these who are members of my family, you have done to me." Matthew 25:40

...nd still, and see the victory of the LORD on your ...alf. 2 Chronicles 20:17

"God Is Working" by the Brooklyn Tabernacle Choir (*God Is Working—Live* ©2000, Sony/Word)

...s Christ says: "The Advocate, the Holy Spirit, ...om the Father will send in my name, will teach you ...rything, and remind you of all that I have said to ..." John 14:26

"All Things Are Possible" (*WoW Worship Green* ©2001, Sony/Epic)

...ereign God, thank you that your victory means ...dom for us. God, help us to acknowledge you in ...y area in our lives. Teach us, Holy Spirit, and ...ind us of tips you have given us to make it through ... Amen

WEEK 35

monday

Psalm 103:19-22

Judges 8:1-35; Luke 20:9-19

...h found favor before the LORD. Genesis 6:8

"The Change" by Steven Curtis Chapman (*Speechless* ©1999, EMD/Sparrow)

...aith Noah respected the warning and built an ark ...ave his household; by this he condemned the ...d and became an heir to the righteousness that is ...ccordance with faith. Hebrews 11:7

"So Good to Me" by Darryl Evans (*Freedom* ©1999, Word)

...er, we want to know your Word so that we may ...w in your ways. God, we ask for your favor in ...relationships, in our studies and work, and in our ...ionship with you. We rejoice in who you are and ...ur goodness to us. Amen

WEEK 35

■ Psalm 104:1-9
■ Judges 9:1-33; Luke 20:20-26

I am coming to gather all nations and tongues; and they shall come and see my glory. Isaiah 66:18

> "Smell the Color Nine" by Chris Rice (*Smell the Color Nine* ©2000, Sony/Word)

All of them were filled with the Holy Spirit and began to speak in other languages, as the Spirit gave them ability. Acts 2:4

> "Deep Enough to Dream" by Chris Rice (*Deep Enough to Dream* ©1997, Sony/Word)

God, there is something so marvelous in your plan to gather the nations. Each person helps to bring a reflection of your glory. Holy Spirit, it is our prayer that you would glorify the Father through our life, actions, and words. Amen

WEEK 35

■ Psalm 104:10-18
■ Judges 9:34—10:18; Luke 20:27-40

Let your face shine upon your desolated sanctuary. Daniel 9:17

> "Shine" by the Newsboys (*Shine...The Hits* ©2000, EMD/Sparrow)

Like living stones, let yourselves be built into a spiritual house, to be a holy priesthood, to offer spiritual sacrifices acceptable to God through Jesus Christ. 1 Peter 2:5

> "Into Jesus" by dc Talk (*WoW 1999* ©1998, EMD/Chordant)

Lord Jesus, we recognize that sanctification is a process. We give our life to you Lord, that you would begin to wash away the impurities and make us holy, so that one day we can stand as your bride, without spot or blemish. Amen

■ Psalm 104:19-23
   Judges 11:1-27; Luke 20:41—21:4

...oses said: "If I, LORD, have found favor in your ...ht, O LORD, I pray, let the LORD go with us." ...odus 34:9

"Better Is One Day" by Passion Worship Band (*Better Is One Day* ©2000, EMD/Sparrow)

...ul wrote: "I live, yet not I, but Christ lives in me." ...atians 2:20

"Big House" by Audio Adrenaline (*Hit Parade* ©2001, EMD/Chordant)

...her, your presence means so much that we don't ...nt to go anywhere without it! Lord, we want to ...ell in your house all the time. Holy Spirit, we pray ...t you would always be changing us into the image ...Christ, and that our testimony would impact ...ers. Amen

■ Psalm 104:24-30
   Judges 11:28—12:15; Luke 21:5-28

...s God forgotten to be gracious? Has he in anger ...t up his compassion? Psalm 77:9

"Peace" (*Rejoice Africa* ©Hosanna! For more information click on www.integritymusic.com)

...us answered: "Neither this man nor his parents ...e sinned, he was born blind so that the works of ...d might be revealed in him." John 9:3

"Open the Eyes of My Heart" (*WoW Worship—Today's 30 Most Powerful Worship Songs* ©1999, Sony/Word)

...d, we pray that our circumstances would not block ...perception of who you really are. No matter what ...pens, Lord, you are always the same God, faithful ...compassionate. Have mercy on us, Lord, and ...t us favor. Amen

WEEK 35

▰▰ Psalm 104:31-35
▰▰ Judges 13:1-25; Luke 21:29-38

Say to those of a fearful heart: "Be strong, do not fear! Here is your God." Isaiah 35:4

> "My Deliverer" by Rich Mullins and the Ragamuffin Band (*Jesus Record* ©1998, Sony/Word)

Christ spoke: "I am the Alpha and the Omega, the beginning and the end. To the thirsty I will give water as a gift from the spring of the water of life." Revelation 21:6

> "Lord, I Lift Your Name on High" (*WoW Worship—Today's 30 Most Powerful Worship Songs* ©1999, Sony/Word)

Jesus, our comforter, just speaking your name fills us with peace. Thank you, Lord, that your perfect love drives out fear. We want to live all the days of our lives under your protection and goodness. Thank you for loving us. Amen

WEEK 36

Watchword for the Week
Bless the LORD, O my soul, and do not forget all his benefits. Psalm 103:2

Rejoice with Jerusalem, and be glad for her, all you who love her. Rejoice with her in joy, all you who mourn over her. Isaiah 66:10

> "Better Is One Day" by Passion Worship Band (*Better Is One Day* ©2000, EMD/Sparrow)

And I heard a loud voice from the throne saying, "See, the home of God is among mortals. He will dwell with them as their God, they will be his peoples, and God himself will be with them." Revelation 21:3

> "One Like You" by Audio Adrenaline (*Hit Parade* ©2001, ForeFront)

O living God, there is none like you! As we look forward to a life eternal in your kingdom, may we still remember that here and now, you are with us. May we never lose focus of your presence in our lives. Amen

Psalm 105:1-7

Judges 14:1—15:20; Luke 22:1-13

eep far from a false charge. Exodus 23:7

> "Every Time I Fall" by Jaci Velasquez (*Crystal Clear* ©2000, Word)

utting away falsehood, let all of us speak truth to
ur neighbors, for we are members of one another.
phesians 4:25

> "Never Dim" by The Waiting (*The Waiting* ©1997, Sparrow)

loving Shepherd, as we travel through life's ever-
hanging moments, we trust that your hand will
uide and protect us. We thank you for your Spirit,
ho comforts and keeps us strong in the face of our
oubles. Amen

Psalm 105:8-15

Judges 16:1—17:13; Luke 22:14-23

he spirit of God has made me, and the breath of the
lmighty gives me life. Job 33:4

> "Your Love Surrounds Me" by Parkway (*Glad You Made It* ©2000, Essential)

or we are what he has made us, created in Christ
sus for good works, which God prepared before-
and to be our way of life. Ephesians 2:10

> "Colored People" by dc Talk (*Jesus Freak* ©1995, ForeFront)

reator of all life, may we receive gentle reminders
ach day of how important we are to you. May we
me to an understanding of who we are and what
r purpose is; the way you would have us. We give
rselves to you in Jesus' name. Amen

WEEK 36

■ Psalm 105:16-22
■ Judges 18:1-31; Luke 22:24-38

From the rising of the sun to its setting my name is great among the nations, says the LORD of hosts. Malachi 1:11

> "Constant" by Out of the Grey (*See Inside* ©1997, Chordant/Sparrow)

[Jesus Christ said:] "As long as I am in the world, I am the light of the world." John 9:5

> "Let There Be Light" by Pam Thum (*Let There Be...* ©2000, Ministry Music)

Thank you, Lord Jesus, for giving us your light in this world of darkness. May each sunrise and sunset remind us of your constant, abiding love for us. May we reflect your light and share our love with others, sacrificially, the way you have. Amen

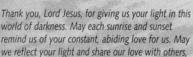

WEEK 36

■ Psalm 105:23-36
■ Judges 19:1-30; Luke 22:39-46

Have you not brought this upon yourself, by forsaking the LORD your God, while he led you in the way? Jeremiah 2:17

> "St. Augustine's Pears" by Petra (*God Fixation* ©1998, Sony/Word)

No one can serve two masters; for a slave will either hate the one and love the other, or be devoted to the one and despise the other. You cannot serve God and wealth. Matthew 6:24

> "Second Hand Clothing Part 2" by Eli (*Second Hand Clothing* ©1999, ForeFront)

Forgiving Father, we know that often we disappoint you with our selfishness and pride. Please humble us once again by covering us with your unfailing grace. May we always remember what you did for us on the cross. In Jesus' life-saving name we pray. Amen

friday

Psalm 105:37-45

Judges 20:1-31; Luke 22:47-62

shall not make wrongful use of the name of the your God, for the LORD will not acquit anyone misuses his name. Exodus 20:7

"Prizm" by PAX217 (*Two Seventeen* ©2000, ForeFront)

e name of Jesus every knee should bend, in en and on earth and under the earth. opians 2:10

"Look What You've Done" by Tree 63 (*Tree 63* ©2000, EMD/Chordant)

od of truth and promise, search our hearts. etimes we don't give you the respect you so ly deserve. Please remove the nonchalant udes from our hearts and minds. Bring us back r to you through your loving discipline. Amen

saturday

Psalm 106:1-5

Judges 20:32—21:25; Luke 22:63-71

give thanks to you, O LORD, for though you angry with me, your anger turned away and you orted me. Isaiah 12:1

"His Love Is Strong" by Clay Crosse (*I Surrender All* ©1999, Reunion)

ever believes in the Son has eternal life; whoever eys the Son will not see life, but must endure s wrath. John 3:36

"Breakfast" by the Newsboys (*Take Me to Your Leader* ©1996, Star Song)

Father, with humble hearts we give you praise ne love and mercy you've given us. We know eternal separation from you is the ultimate ty for our sins, but through your grace we look ard to a life eternal with you in your kingdom. n

WEEK 37

Watchword for the Week
Cast all your anxieties on him, for
he cares for you. 1 Peter 5:7

Alas for those who devise wickedness, and evil deeds
on their beds! Micah 2:1

"Waiting Room" by La Rue (*La Rue* ©1999,
Reunion)

Whoever wishes to become great among you must be
your servant. Mark 10:43

"I Want to Know You" by Sonicflood (*Sonicflood*
©1999, Gotee)

*Dearest Lord, as we journey through life, struggling to
know you more, may your ever-present Spirit give us
comfort and peace. May we receive knowledge of you
beyond what we could ever imagine. In Christ Jesus'
name we pray. Amen*

WEEK 37

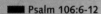

■ Psalm 106:6-12
■ Ruth 1:1-22; Luke 23:1—23:12

O Lord, you are our God, let no mortal prevail
against you. 2 Chronicles 14:11

"God You Are My God" by Delirious? (*Glo*
©2000, Sparrow)

We cannot keep from speaking about what we have
seen and heard. Acts 4:20

"Best Kept Secret" by Skillet (*Invincible* ©2000,
Ardent)

*Father God, we are sorry that we do not share the
good news with others as often as we should. Please
remind us, over and over again, of the price you paid
for our sins. May the joy of our salvation emanate
from our very being. Amen*

■ Psalm 106:13-23
■ Ruth 2:1—3:18; Luke 23:13-31

[LOR]D had made them joyful. Ezra 6:22

"Shout to the Lord" by Darlene Zschech (*I Believe the Promise* ©1998, Integrity/Word)

[re]joice in hope, be patient in suffering, persevere in [pra]yer. Romans 12:12

"Go and Sin No More" by Rebecca St. James (*God* ©1996, ForeFront)

[G]reat Comforter, you are mighty and powerful [bey]ond our comprehension. May we proclaim the joy [tha]t comes from you to the ends of your earth. May [we] stand up, unashamed, feeling the cleansing of [you]r forgiveness. In Jesus' name we pray. Amen

■ Psalm 106:24-31
■ Ruth 4:1-22; Luke 23:32-43

[God] had made them rejoice with great joy; the [wo]men and children also rejoiced. The joy of [Jeru]salem was heard far away. Nehemiah 12:43

"The Real Thing" by World Wide Message Tribe (*Revived* ©1997, Warner Brothers)

[The]y praised God and had the good will of the [peo]ple. Acts 2:47

"God's Been Good to Me" by Crystal Lewis (*Beauty For Ashes* ©1996, Sony/Word)

[Gra]cious One, we know from whom our blessings [flow]. Thank you for the many gifts and privileges you [gr]ow to us every day. May we repay you through [our] faith walk and testimony. Glory be to God [fore]ver! Amen

WEEK 37

▰▰▰ Psalm 106:32-39
▰▰▰ 1 Samuel 1:1—2:11; Luke 23:44-56

You are God, you alone, of all the kingdoms of the earth; you have made heaven and earth. Isaiah 37:16

> "Water" by Matt Brouwer (*Imagerical* ©2001, Reunion)

[Paul wrote:] With the eyes of your heart enlightened, you may know what is the hope to which he has called you, what are the riches of his glorious inheritance among the saints, and what is the immeasurable greatness of his power for us who believe, according to the working of his great power. God put this power to work in Christ. Ephesians 1:18-20

> "Defying Gravity" by John Elefante (*Defying Gravity* ©1999, Pamplin)

O God, our living water, flood us with your grace and forgiveness. May we defy the magnetic pull of this world through your uplifting, loving hand. And with your hand, guide us and strengthen us, so that we may do your will. Amen

WEEK 37

▰▰▰ Psalm 106:40-48
▰▰▰ 1 Samuel 2:12-36; Luke 24:1-12

With weeping they shall come, and with consolations I will lead them back, for I am Israel's Father. Jeremiah 31:9

> "By the Rivers of Babylon" by The Kry (*What About Now* ©1996, Freedom)

So you have pain now, but I will see you again, and your hearts will rejoice, and no one will take your joy from you. John 16:22

> "Walk on Your Knees" by Aaron Jeoffrey (*Aaron Jeoffrey* ©1994, Star Song)

Forgiving Father, we come to you on our knees in the midst of pain, trouble, confusion, and worry. We cry out to you, "Lord, rescue me!" Lead us back to the peace and comfort only your hand can provide. Thank you for your mercy. Amen

WEEK 37

saturday

▩ Psalm 107:1-9
▩ 1 Samuel 3:1—4:22; Luke 24:13-27

The LORD takes pleasure in those who fear him, in those who hope in his steadfast love. Psalm 147:11

| "The Meeting" by Anderson, Bruford, Wakeman, and Howe (*Anderson Bruford Wakeman and Howe* ©1989, Arista)

He said to her: "Daughter, your faith has made you well; go in peace, and be healed of your disease." Mark 5:34

| "Hold Me Jesus" by Rich Mullins (*A Liturgy, a Legacy, and a Ragamuffin Band* ©1993, Reunion)

Keeper of our souls, in the meeting of your love, we surrender and lay aside our selfish desires and agendas. Although the act of surrender is frightening at times, we trust that you are in control. Help strengthen our faith. In Jesus' powerful name we pray. Amen

---

WEEK 38

sunday

Watchword for the Week
It has now been revealed through the appearing of our Savior Christ Jesus, who abolished death and brought life and immortality to light through the gospel. 2 Timothy 1:10

When the wicked turn away from the wickedness they have committed and do what is lawful and right, they shall save their life. Ezekiel 18:27

| "Change My Heart, Oh God" (*WoW Worship— Today's 30 Most Powerful Worship* ©1999, Sony/Word)

Paul wrote: "They only heard it said, 'The one who formerly was persecuting us is now proclaiming the faith he once tried to destroy.' And they glorified God because of me." Galatians 1:23-24

| "I Will Never Be" (*Shout to the Lord* ©1998, Sony/Word)

Heavenly Father, as we come to you and ask your forgiveness, you turn your back to what has gone before and cast your eyes on what will be. When we turn our lives over to you, you turn our lives around that it may bring glory to you. Amen

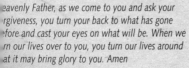

WEEK 38

▬ Psalm 107:10-16
▬ 1 Samuel 5:1—7:1; Luke 24:28-35

Worship the LORD with gladness; come into his presence with singing. Psalm 100:2

> 'Shout to the Lord" by Hillsongs (*Shout to the Lord-Platinum Collection* ©2000, Sony/Word)

For it is the God who said, "Let light shine out of darkness," who has shone in our hearts to give the light of the knowledge of the glory of God in the face of Jesus Christ. 2 Corinthians 4:6

> "In the Light" by dc Talk (*Jesus Freak* ©1995, EMD/Chordant)

Lord, you have opened the door to the room of our hearts letting your light pour into its darkest corners. Because of this we worship you with infinite joy. Jesus, your face has shone on us and shown us the glory of God. Amen

---

WEEK 38

tuesday

▬ Psalm 107:17-22
▬ 1 Samuel 7:2—8:22; Luke 24:36-53

He raises up the poor from the dust. 1 Samuel 2:8

> "Humble Thyself" (*Generation Praise* ©1999. For more information click on www.generationpraise.com)

So I tell you, whatever you ask for in prayer, believe that you have received it, and it will be yours. Mark 11:24

> "Hard to Get" by Rich Mullins (*The Jesus Record* ©1998, Reunion)

Mighty God, bring us to our knees in fervent and expectant prayer. We come into your presence by faith seeking to be broken and humbled, knowing when we rise we will find your answer. Amen

wednesday

Psalm 107:23-32

1 Samuel 9:1-27; John 1:1-13

e tested you in the furnace of adversity.
h 48:10

"Lead of Love" by Caedmon's Call (*Caedmon's
Call* ©1997, Warner Alliance)

at moment, while he was still speaking, the cock
ed. The Lord turned and looked at Peter. Then
remembered the word of the Lord, how he had
to him, "Before the cock crows today, you will
me three times" And he went out and wept
ly. Luke 22:60-62

"This Is Your Time" by Michael W. Smith (*This
Is Your Time* ©1999, Reunion)

*g God, you have the power to redeem even our
est situations, our deepest betrayals, our most
dful mistakes. Through our sorrow and tears, we
our light shining. Your glory triumphs over death
we are humbled by this great mystery. Amen*

thursday

Psalm 107:33-43

1 Samuel 10:1-27; John 1:14-28

saw how the LORD your God carried you, just as
carries a child. Deuteronomy 1:31

"You're Here" by Sixpence None the Richer
(*City on a Hill* ©2000, Squint)

not cease to give thanks for you as I remembered
n my prayers. I pray that the God of our Lord
Christ, the Father of glory, may give you a spirit
sdom and revelation as you come to know him.
sians 1:16-17

"Love Song for a Savior" by Jars of Clay (*Jars of
Clay* ©1995, BMG/Jive/Silvertone)

*Father. You carry us close to you and we curl
ke a child in your arms. We feel your restoring
ace, but like a good parent we feel you chal-
ng us to grow, to walk beside you and learn
you as you reveal yourself to us. Amen*

WEEK 38

■ Psalm 108:1-5
■ Samuel 11:1—12:25; John 1:29-34

I blessed the Most High, and praised and honored the one who lives forever. For his sovereignty is an everlasting sovereignty, and his kingdom endures from generation to generation. All the inhabitants of the earth are accounted as nothing. Daniel 4:34-35

> "Ancient of Days" (WoW Worship—Today's 30 Most Powerful Worship Songs ©1999, Sony/Word)

Jesus answered Pilate: "You would have no power over me, if it were not given to you from above." John 19:11

> "Agnus Dei" by Third Day (Exodus ©1998, Sony/Word)

Holy God, you stand alone, reigning supreme over time and space. There is nothing and no one who compares with you. We find complete rest knowing that all power and authority belong to you. We are nothing, Lord, but through your Son we have everything. Amen

WEEK 38

■ Psalm 108:6-13
■ 1 Samuel 13:1-23; John 1:35-51

My heart and my flesh sing for joy to the living God. Psalm 84:2

> "I Could Sing of Your Love Forever" by Delirious? (Cutting Edge ©1997, EMD/Sparrow)

Although you have not seen him, you love him; and even though you do not see him now, you believe in him and rejoice with an indescribable and glorious joy, for you are receiving the outcome of your faith, the salvation of your souls. 1 Peter 1:8-9

> "I Love You Lord" by Any Given Day (Passionate Worship for the Soul ©2001, EMD/Chordant)

Living God, a rush of praises flood our bodies and souls because we hear your voice and see you working in your world. We sing endless love songs to you, who has loved us all enough to deliver us from our sin. Amen

sunday

Watchword for the Week

And this is the victory that conquers the world, our faith. 1 John 5:4

d, "I will guard my ways that I may not sin with tongue." Psalm 39:1

"Between You and Me" by dc Talk (*Jesus Freak* ©1995, EMD/Chordant)

us love, not in word or speech, but in truth and on. 1 John 3:18

"Know My Heart" by Sara Groves (*Conversations* ©2001, Sony/Word)

iving Father, we confess to you that our motives not always pure. The truth we profess is not ays found to be true in the way we live our lives. n our actions with our words. Help us to follow that your love might flow through us. Amen

monday

Psalm 109:1-7
1 Samuel 14:1-40; John 2:1-11

my heart to your decrees, and not to selfish gain. m 119:36

"Where You Belong/Turn Your Eyes upon Jesus" by the Newsboys (*Shine...the Hits* ©2000, EMD/Sparrow)

spoke to the farmer: "You fool! This very night life is being demanded of you. And the things have prepared, whose will they be?" Luke 12:20

"Worlds Apart" by Jars of Clay (*Jars of Clay* ©1995, BMG/Jive/Silvertone)

, we confess that we often confuse your abun-
e with our own, grasping it tightly. Loosen our
Lord. Help us to become servants like you and
onger slaves to our selfishness. Change us. Amen

WEEK 39

■■■ Psalm 109:8-20
■■■ 1 Samuel 14:41—15:23;
John 2:12-25

The days are surely coming, says the LORD, when I will make a new covenant with the house of Israel and the house of Judah. Jeremiah 31:31

> "Covenant Song" by Caedmon's Call (*City on the Hill* ©2000, BMG/Jive/Silvertone)

Christ is the mediator of the new covenant, so that those who are called may receive the promised eternal inheritance, because a death has occurred that redeems them from the transgressions under the first covenant. Hebrews 9:15

> "God So Loved" by Jaci Velasquez (*Jaci Velasquez* ©1998, Myrrh Records)

Lord God, you sent your Son to live and die for us. You altered the course of our lives. We were drowning under the weight of our failures and you—the very one we have failed—have lifted us up. Thank you, Lord. Amen

WEEK 39

■■■ Psalm 109:21-31
■■■ 1 Samuel 15:24—16:13; John 3:1-15

How weighty to me are your thoughts, O God! How vast is the sum of them! Psalm 139:17

> "Be Magnified" by Radical for Christ (*Praise in the House* ©1996, Sony/Word)

Look at the birds of the air; they neither sow nor reap nor gather into barns, and yet your heavenly Father feeds them. Are you not of more value than they? Matthew 6:26

> "I Know Your Name" by Michael W. Smith (*Live the Life* ©1998, BMG/Jive/Silvertone)

God, sometimes it seems that we try so hard to contain you, to melt you down into something we can swallow. How incredible it is, Lord, that you in your greatness have created us and adore us. May our image of you expand. Amen

Psalm 110

1 Samuel 16:14—17:31; John 3:16-26

he eyes of all look to you, and you give them their
od in due season. You open your hand satisfying
e desire of every living thing. Psalm 145:15-16

| "Can't Live a Day" by Avalon (*In a Different
Light* ©1999, Sparrow)

sus spoke to them: "I am the bread of life. Whoever
omes to me shall never hunger; and whoever
elieves in me shall never thirst." John 6:35

| "Thirsty" by Chris Rice (*Past the Edges* ©1998,
Rocketown)

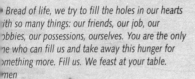

*Bread of life, we try to fill the holes in our hearts
ith so many things: our friends, our job, our
obbies, our possessions, ourselves. You are the only
ne who can fill us and take away this hunger for
omething more. Fill us. We feast at your table.
men*

Psalm 111

1 Samuel 17:32-58; John 3:27-36

ay you have a full reward from the LORD, the God
Israel, under whose wings you have come for
fuge. Ruth 2:12

| "How Deep the Father's Love for Us" by Skillet
(*Ardent Worship: Skillet Live* ©2000, Chordant)

here is salvation in no one else, for there is no other
ame under heaven given among mortals by which
e must be saved. Acts 4:12

| "Love Song for a Savior" by Jars of Clay (*Jars of
Clay* ©1995, BMG/Jive/Silvertone)

*ctorious Lord, the reward of our salvation does not
ake sense. You won the race and we get the prize.
ou took our place, Lord, trading your sin-free life for
ur shameful one. Praise and honor to your precious
me. Amen*

WEEK 39

■■ Psalm 112
■■ 1 Samuel 18:1—19:7; John 4:1-26

For the LORD your God is a devouring fire, a jealous God. Deuteronomy 4:24

> "Consume Me" by dc Talk (*Supernatural* ©1998, EMD/Virgin)

Therefore, since we are receiving a kingdom that cannot be shaken, let us give thanks, by which we offer to God an acceptable worship with reverence and awe. Hebrews 12:28

> "I Stand in Awe" by Any Given Day (*Passionate Worship for the Soul* ©2001, EMD/Chordant)

Unshakeable Creator, we marvel at your creation—the glory of the stars and the beauty of the earth—but we desire a heart that is even more in awe of you. Devour our hearts with your fire, Lord, that there may be no room left for anything but you. Amen

WEEK 40

Watchword for the Week
The angel of the LORD encamps around those who fear him, and delivers them. Psalm 34:7

For I give water in the wilderness, rivers in the desert, to give drink to my chosen people. Isaiah 43:20

> "As the Deer" by Brain Duncan (*My Utmost for His Highest* ©1996, Sony/Word)

There appeared an angel to him from heaven and strengthened him. Luke 22:43

> "This Road" by Jars of Clay (*City on a Hill* ©2000, BMG/Jive/Silvertone)

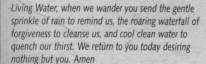

Living Water, when we wander you send the gentle sprinkle of rain to remind us, the roaring waterfall of forgiveness to cleanse us, and cool clean water to quench our thirst. We return to you today desiring nothing but you. Amen

monday

Psalm 113
1 Samuel 19:8—20:17; John 4:27-38

you not known? Have you not heard? The LORD
everlasting God, the Creator of the ends of the
He does not grow weary; his understanding is
rchable. Isaiah 40:28

"I Know You Know" by Sierra (WoW 1997
©1996, EMD/Chordant)

rist are hidden all the treasures of wisdom and
ledge. Colossians 2:3

"You Are My All in All" by Dennis Jernigan
(Vol.2 You Are My All in All ©1990, Provident)

esus, in you we have been given a treasure
d what we can comprehend. We are tired but
ever grow weary. We get confused but you
stand it all. There is so much we don't know,
l wisdom and knowledge is found in you. Your
and your plans are perfect. Amen

tuesday

Psalm 114
1 Samuel 20:18—21:9; John 4:39-42

rtal, born of woman, is few of days and full of
e. Job 14:1

"Romans" by Jennifer Knapp (Kansas ©1998,
EMD/Chordant)

said: "Take my yoke upon you and learn from
or I am gentle and humble in heart, and you will
est for your souls." Matthew 11:29

"Rain On" by Brother's Keeper (Brother's
Keeper ©1999, EMD/Chordant)

st Lord, thank you so much for always being
for us in times of trouble. You know that our
down here on earth are never easy, but you are
s faithful to us and will always be there to pick
. We praise you, Lord, for all that you do for us.

WEEK 40

■ **Psalm 115:1-8**
■ **1 Samuel 21:10—22:23; John 4:43-54**

Your sins have deprived you of good. Jeremiah 5:25

> "Free" by Steven Curtis Chapman (*Signs of Life*
> ©1996, EMD/Sparrow)

If you then, who are evil, know how to give good
gifts to your children, how much more will the heavenly Father give the Holy Spirit to those who ask him!
Luke 11:13

> "More Faithful" by Skillet (*Hey You, I Love Your*
> *Soul* ©1998, Photon Music)

Good Father, we know that our sins keep us from
your blessings of freedom and peace. Please give us
strength to overcome our sinfulness through Jesus so
that we are no longer slaves to sin, but free in the
Son. Thank you so much for the liberation from sin
that you give us. Amen

WEEK 40

■ **Psalm 115:9-18**
■ **1 Samuel 23:1-29; John 5:1-15**

David spoke to his son Solomon: "Be strong, be
courageous, and serve the LORD, your God."
1 Kings 2:2-3

> "My Will" by dc Talk (*Exodus* ©1998,
> Rocketown)

Whoever serves me, the Father will honor. John 12:26

> "Hands and Feet" by Audio Adrenaline
> (*Underdog* ©1999, ForeFront)

Awesome Father, thank you so much for giving us the
chance to serve you. Give us strength to endure any-
thing that might be a stumbling block as we work to
do your will. Thank you for all the blessings you will
give us as we make every effort to do what pleases
you. Amen

EEK 40

friday

Psalm 116:1-7
1 Samuel 24:1—25:17; John 5:16-30

LORD says: "If you turn back, I will take you
." Jeremiah 15:19

"Take You at Your Word" by Avalon (*In a
Different Light* ©1999, EMD/Sparrow)

answered him: "Those who love me will keep
vord, and my Father will love them, and we will
e to them and make our home with them."
14:23

"Draw Me Close to You" by The Katinas
(*Exodus* ©1998, Rocketown)

er God, we know that relationships always take
t on both parts. It is amazing how faithful you
Thank you for always being dependable even
n we are not. Give us the strength and
rnment to make the right decisions to be faithful
ou always. Amen

EEK 40

saturday

Psalm 116:8-14
1 Samuel 25:18-44; John 5:31-47

LORD gives the sun for light by day and the stars
ght by night; he stirs up the sea so that its waves
Jeremiah 31:35

"These Thousand Hills" by Third Day
(*Offerings: A Worship Album* ©2000,
BMG/Brentwood)

areful then how you live, not as unwise people
as wise. Ephesians 5:15

"Things I Prayed For" by Eli (*Things I Prayed
For* ©1998, EMD/Chordant)

cious Father, thank you so much for the beautiful
h you created for us. Help us to remember to take
of it and be wise in the life-choices we make.
us to pray for the things that will be pleasing to
Amen

WEEK 41

Watchword for the Week
The eyes of all look to you, and you give them their food in due season. Psalm 145:15

Commit your way to the LORD, trust in him and he will act. Psalm 37:5

> "God Is Watching over You" by Phil Joel (*Watching over You* ©2000, EMD/Chordant)

When he has brought out all his own, he goes ahead of them, and the sheep follow him because they know his voice. John 10:4

> "Needful Hands" by Jars of Clay (*Exodus* ©1998, Rocketown)

Good Shepherd, guide us daily in all that we do. We do not know the way to live without you. We do not know the path of righteousness. Lead us in the way that is right and just in your sight. Amen

---

WEEK 41

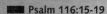 Psalm 116:15-19
1 Samuel 26:1—27:12; John 6:1-15

I will make a covenant of peace with you. Ezekiel 34:25

> "My Deliverer" by Rich Mullins and the Ragamuffin Band (*The Jesus Record* ©1998, Sony/Word)

Blessed be the Lord God of Israel, for he has looked favorably on his people and redeemed them. He has shown the mercy promised to our ancestors and has remembered his holy covenant. Luke 1:68, 72

> "Unforgetful You" by Jars of Clay (*If I Left the Zoo* ©1999, BMG/Jive/Novus/Silvertone)

Thank you, almighty Father, for being so faithful to us. You never break your promises. You have redeemed us and blessed us with your peace. May we always praise you for all that you do. Amen

tuesday

Psalm 117

1 Samuel 28:1—29:11; John 6:16-24

I any pleasure in the death of the wicked, says ORD God, and not rather that they should turn their ways and live? Ezekiel 18:23

"Entertaining Angels" by the Newsboys (*Step Up to the Microphone* ©1998, Star Song)

s said:] "There will be more rejoicing in heaven one sinner who repents than ninety-nine right- people." Luke 15:7

"Go and Sin No More" by Rebecca St. James (*Pray* ©1998, EMD/Chordant)

of love, thank you so much for always giving us hance to come back to you after we go astray. love for us is astonishing—you will take us back we constantly betray you. Give us the strength o fall from you, and the wisdom to know when ave. Amen

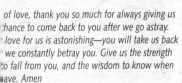

wednesday

Psalm 118:1-9

1 Samuel 30:1-31; John 6:25-41

y are the afflictions of the righteous, but the LORD es them from them all. Psalm 34:19

"Where There Is Faith" by 4Him (*Best Ones* ©1999, BMG/Verity)

hope for you is unshaken; for we know that as share in our sufferings, so also you share in our olation. 2 Corinthians 1:7

"Grand Scheme" by Solomon's Wish (*A Wise Man's Tragedy...* ©1999, Pamplin)

hful Father, we praise you for always being a derful friend. Thank you for always giving us ngth and courage when things are hard. Your love ds our spirit daily. Amen

WEEK 41

thursda

▬ Psalm 118:10-14
▬ 1 Samuel 31:1-13; 2 Samuel 1:1-27;
John 6:42-46

At that time I will change the speech of the peoples to
a pure speech, that all of them may call on the name
of the LORD and serve him with one accord.
Zephaniah 3:9

> "I Could Sing of Your Love Forever" by
> Sonicflood (*Sonicflood* ©1999, EMD/Chordant)

Through him, then, let us continually offer a sacrifice
of praise to God, that is, the fruit of lips that confess
his name. Hebrews 13:15

> "When I Praise" by Ffh (*Found a Place* ©2000,
> Reunion)

*Glorious Father, we praise you with our lives. Let our
speech be pleasing to your ears. Let our actions speak
your praise to everyone around us. May we do all
that is in our might to let others know of your
wonderful love. Amen*

WEEK 41

friday

▬ Psalm 118:15-21
▬ 2 Samuel 2:1-32; John 6:47-59

He is the living God, enduring forever. His kingdom
shall never be destroyed. Daniel 6:26

> "Red Letters" by dc Talk (*Supernatural* ©1998,
> EMD/Virgin)

After his suffering he presented himself alive to them
by many convincing proofs, appearing to them during
forty days and speaking about the kingdom of God.
Acts 1:3

> "Ultimate Man" by Nickel & Dime (*3 Days in
> March* ©1996, Nickel & Dime. Click on
> www.nickelanddime.com/home/home.html)

*Everlasting Father, your kingdom is so awesome. Your
glory shines all around. Shine it down on us and fill
us with your Spirit. Free us from our sins, so that we
may share in your marvelous kingdom, Amen*

saturday

Psalm 118:22-29
2 Samuel 3:1-34; John 6:60-71

the pillars of the earth are the LORD's, and on
n he has set the world. 1 Samuel 2:8

"The Solid Rock" by 4Him (*Hymns—A Place of
Worship* ©2000, BMG/Verity)

no one can lay any foundation other than the one
he has been laid; that foundation is Jesus Christ.
orinthians 3:11

"The Stone" by Jars of Clay (*City on a Hill*
©2000, BMG/Jive/Novus/Silvertone)

dfast Father, we thank you for the strong founda-
s you have shown us in your Word. Build up a
ndation in us, that we may grow strong in your
it. Amen

sunday

Watchword for the Week

He has told you, O mortal, what is
good; and what does the LORD
require of you, but to do justice,
and to love kindness, and to walk
humbly with your God. Micah 6:8

have put gladness in my heart more than when
grain and wine abound. Psalm 4:7

"There You Go" by Caedmon's Call (*40 Acres*
©1999, Cumbee Road)

does God's love abide in anyone who has the
d's goods and sees a brother or sister in need and
efuses help? 1 John 3:17

"Jesus to the World" by Newsong (*Arise My
Love...The Best of Newsong* ©2000, Reunion)

est Lord, your joy is better than any that we can
on the earth. Help us to share that joy with oth-
and be a joyful servant of yours to everyone we
, so they may know you as well. Amen

WEEK 42

Psalm 119:1-8
2 Samuel 3:35—5:16; John 7:1-13

[Jeremiah said:] "My heart is sick, for the hurt of my poor people I am hurt, is there no physician there?" Jeremiah 8:18, 21-22.

> "Your Love (Keeps Me Alive)" by Skillet (*Hey You, I Love Your Soul* ©1998, Photon)

The power of the Lord was with Jesus to heal. Luke 5:17

> "Under Bridges" by Brave Saint Saturn (*So Far from Home* ©2000, EMD/Five Minute Walk)

Wonderful Healer, cleanse us from all our sin and heal our aching hearts. You are the great physician, and only you can heal us from any hurt that we may feel. Thank you for your comfort when we feel sick, both physically and spiritually. Amen

WEEK 42

Psalm 119:9-16
2 Samuel 5:17—6:23; John 7:14-24

He is a shield for all who take refuge in him. Psalm 18:30

> "My Hope Is You" by Third Day (*Conspiracy #5* ©1997, BMG/Jive/Silvertone)

The Lord is faithful; he will strengthen you and guard you from the evil one. 2 Thessalonians 3:3

> "Unfazed" by The Waiting (*Unfazed* ©1999, EMD/Sparrow)

Thank you, Lord, for always being so faithful to us. Your love strengthens us through the tough times. Your Spirit gives us courage in times of fear. Keep us strong, Father, when we are weak so that we may always stand up against evil. Amen

wednesday

Psalm 119:17-24
2 Samuel 7:1-29; John 7:25-43

not be afraid, stand firm, and see the deliverance
the LORD will accomplish for you today.
...dus 14:13

"The Only Thing I Need" by 4Him (*Dove
Award Nominees & Winners: Best Of 2000*
©2000, Pamplin)

...hat you heard from the beginning abides in you,
...you will abide in the Son and in the Father.
...hn 2:24

"Stand" by Bebo Norman (*Ten Thousand Days*
©1999, BMG/Brentwood)

...at Comforter, thank you for always being there for
...when we are afraid or unsure. May your Spirit
...ays abide in us as we work hard to do your will.
...en

---

thursday

Psalm 119:25-32
2 Samuel 8:1—9:13; John 7:44-53

...we have heard, so we have seen in the city of the
...D of hosts, which God establishes forever.
...m 48:8

"The New Jerusalem" by Michael Card
(*Unveiled Hope* ©1997, Myrrh)

...w the holy city, the new Jerusalem, coming down
...of heaven from God, prepared as a bride adorned
...her husband. Revelation 21:2

"Come As a Bridegroom" by Dennis Jernigan (*I
Belong to Jesus* ©2000, Here to Him)

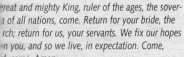

...reat and mighty King, ruler of the ages, the sover-
...of all nations, come. Return for your bride, the
...rch; return for us, your servants. We fix our hopes
...n you, and so we live, in expectation. Come,
...d, come. Amen

WEEK 42

■■ **Psalm 119:33-40**
■■ **2 Samuel 10:1—11:27; John 8:1-11**

The word is very near to you; it is in your mouth and in your heart for you to observe. Deuteronomy 30:14

| "Hands and Feet" by Audio Adrenaline (*Underdog* ©1999, Up in the Mix)

[Paul wrote:] "Pray also for me, so that when I speak, a message may be given to me to make known with boldness the mystery of the gospel." Ephesians 6:19

| "Mirror" by Rebecca St. James (*Pray* ©1998, Forefront)

Master of all time, make us beautiful in your eyes; make us effective in your service. Mold us. Shape the words in our mouths; form the thoughts of our hearts; transform us, Lord. We offer ourselves to you, do as you please. Amen

WEEK 42

■■ **Psalm 119:41-48**
■■ **2 Samuel 12:1-31; John 8:12-30**

God is not a human being that he should lie. Numbers 23:19

| "You Are God" (*WoW Worship Orange* ©2000, Sony/Word)

[Jesus said:] "God is spirit, and those who worship him must worship him in spirit and truth." John 4:24

| "All the Heavens" by Third Day (*Offerings* ©2000, BMG/Jive/Silvertone)

God we praise you. We worship you for who you are, for what you have done, for how you have changed us. Our minds are filled with thanksgiving. Our hearts overflow with praise. Remind us of your glory. Renew us for your work so that we might live in your grace. Amen

sunday

Watchword for the Week

Do not be overcome by evil, but
overcome evil with good.
Romans 12:21

hand laid the foundation of the earth, and my right
d spread out the heavens; when I summon them,
stand at attention. Isaiah 48:13

"Father of Creation" by Darlene Zschech (*Shout
to the Lord* ©1998, Sony/Word)

he beginning was the Word, and the Word was
God, and the Word was God. All things came into
g through him, and without him not one thing
e into being. John 1:1, 3

"Universe" by Rebecca St. James (*Transform*
©2000, EMD/Chordant)

ator of the universe, author of the skies, craftsman
e world, the nations kneel before your throne. We
to revere you as we ought, for you are worthy of
raise. Your ways amaze us. Be patient with your
ants, for we will worship you. Amen

monday

Psalm 119:49-56
2 Samuel 13:1-22; John 8:31-41

people that walked in darkness, have seen a great
; those who lived in a land of deep darkness—on
light has shined. Isaiah 9:2

"I've Always Loved You" by Third Day (*Time*
©1999, Essential)

are a chosen race, a royal priesthood, a holy
on, God's own people, in order that you may pro-
m the mighty acts of him who called you out of
kness into his marvelous light. 1 Peter 2:9

"Under Your Mercy" by Skypark (*Overbluecity*
©2000, Sony/Word)

reat Redeemer, how can this be? What was once
is now light; that which was filthy has become
n. This rotting flesh has been made pure, and
we stand blameless in your sight. Why have you
sen us? Oh, that we might praise you! And so we
Amen

WEEK 43

▰▰ Psalm 119:57-64
▰▰ 2 Samuel 13:23—14:33; John 8:42-59

Now if you are unwilling to serve the LORD, choose this day whom you will serve...But as for me and my house, we will serve the LORD. Joshua 24:15

| "Live for You" by Big Tent Revival (*Choose Life* ©1999, Ardent)

Whoever serves me must follow me, and where I am, there will my servant be. John 12:26

| "Use Me Here" by Everybodyduck (for more information click on www.jamsline.com/b_duck.html)

Yes, Lord, we will follow! We will serve you, for we are yours. But Lord, help us! We are weak, God, our strength is so frail; our hearts so wavering; our desires so scattered. Hold us. Surround us. And use us. Yes, Lord. We will follow! Amen

WEEK 43

▰▰ Psalm 119:65-72
▰▰ 2 Samuel 15:1-37; John 9:1-12

My mouth is filled with your praise, and with your glory all day long. Psalm 71:8

| "Let Everything That Has Breath" (*Passion: Better Is One Day* ©2000, Sparrow)

Let no evil talk come out of your mouths, but only what is useful for building up, as there is need, so that your words may give grace to those who hear. Ephesians 4:29

| "With Every Breath" (*City on a Hill* ©2000, Essential)

Bind our tongues, shape our words, Father, for we desire to honor you in our speech. But even more, resurrect our minds, for our thoughts must first be heavenward. And now, Lord, renovate our hearts that we might desire you above all else. May the entirety of our lives bring you glory. Amen

◀ Psalm 119:73-80
◀ 2 Samuel 16:1-14; John 9:13-34

s says the LORD: "I will rejoice in doing good to
." Jeremiah 32:36, 41

"Hallelujah" by The Supertones (*Chase the Sun*
©1999, EMD/BEC)

God so loved the world that he gave his only Son,
at everyone who believes in him may not perish
may have eternal life. John 3:16

"Deep and Wide" by The Kry (*Let Me Say*
©2000, Freedom Records)

ciful Lord, you have saved us; you have given us
We had nothing and deserved even less, yet you
hed down from heaven and paid the ultimate
, because you are good. How we want to praise
Take our all, for you are good. Amen

◀ Psalm 119:81-88
◀ 2 Samuel 16:15—17:29; John 9:35-41

not be wise in your own eyes; fear the LORD, and
away from evil. Proverbs 3:7

"Needful Hands" by Jars of Clay (*Exodus*
©1998, Rocketown)

o is wise and understanding among you? Show by
r good life that your works are done with gentle-
born of wisdom. James 3:13

"Walk with the Wise" by Stephen Curtis
Chapman (*The Great Adventure* ©1992,
Sparrow)

wisdom begins with you, Lord, for you are the
t teacher. All understanding is an extension of
r grace, for you have created everything. Light our
s that we might walk with you. Direct us; for we
lost without you. We need you so much; guide
Amen

WEEK 43

■■■ Psalm 119:89-96
■■■ 2 Samuel 18:1-33; John 10:1-6

The LORD has been mindful to us; he will bless us.
Psalms 115:12

> "Speechless" by Steven Curtis Chapman
> (*Speechless* ©1999, Sparrow Records)

Ground that drinks up rain falling on it repeatedly, and
that produces a crop useful to those for whom it is
cultivated, receives a blessing from God. Hebrews 6:7

> "Send Your Rain" Passion Worship Band (*Live
> Worship from the 268 Generation* ©1998, Star
> Song/Chordant)

*Father, you have blessed us. You have given us Christ,
the perfect gift. Nothing could be more special.
Nothing could have such an effect. Yet we find ourselves still wanting...waiting...for what? To know
you more! We want more of you today. Bless us with
your presence. Amen*

WEEK 44

Watchword for the Week
But there is forgiveness with you, so
that you may be revered.
Psalm 130:4

Even youths will faint and be weary, and the young will
fall exhausted; but those who wait for the LORD shall
renew their strength, they shall mount up with wings
like eagles, they shall run and not be weary, they shall
walk and not be faint. Isaiah 40:30-31

> "Breathe" (*Hungry* ©2001, EMD/Chordant)

Paul wrote: "It is God who is at work in you, enabling
you both to will and to work for his good pleasure."
Philippians 2:13

> "With God" by Salvador (*Salvador* ©2000,
> Myrrh/Sony/Word)

*Our Provider, we will wait for you, for you are the
source of our lives. Be our sustenance, our portion.
Give us the strength to go on, to live each day mindful
of the sacrifice you made, that we might have life.
Father, you are all that we need. Amen*

■ **Psalm 119:97-104**
■ **2 Samuel 19:1-23; John 10:7-21**

Most High is your dwelling place. Psalm 91:9

■ "My Refuge" by Sonicflood (*Sonicflood* ©1999, Gotee/EMD/Chordant)

who have taken refuge shall be strongly encour-
 to seize the hope before us. Hebrews 6:18

■ "Down with the Ship" by Seven Day Jesus (*Seven Day Jesus* ©1997, ForeFront)

ighty God, you are so huge! Our understanding
ou seems so faint, yet you seem so near. Your
s are too great to fathom, yet your grace is our
fort. We will rest in the shade of your right hand,
you are our God. Amen

■ **Psalm 119:105-112**
■ **2 Samuel 19:24—20:26;**
 n 10:22-33

shall eat there in the presence of the LORD your
, you and your households together, rejoicing in
he undertakings in which the LORD your God has
sed you. Deuteronomy 12:7

■ "Holy Roar" by Passion Worship Band (*Passion: The Road to One Day* ©2000, Star Song/EMD/Sparrow)

the fatted calf and kill it, and let us eat and cele-
e; for this son of mine was dead and is alive
n; he was lost and is found! And they began to
brate. Luke 15:23-24

■ "A Man after Your Own Heart" by Gary Chapman (*Thirty Years of Award Winning Music* ©1999, BMG/Brentwood)

er, you have done so much! We were lost, reeling
ur sin, groping in the darkness. You grabbed us,
hed us, and restored our souls. May our lives be a
bration of your goodness to us for all the world
ee. Amen

WEEK 44

■ Psalm 119:113-120
■ 2 Samuel 21:1-22; John 10:34-42

The LORD is good to all, and his compassion is over all that he has made. Psalm 145:9

> "Say You Need Love" by Newsboys (*Love Liberty Disco* ©1999, EMD/Chordant/Sparrow)

[Paul wrote:] "He was so ill that he nearly died. But God had mercy upon him, and not only on him but on me also, so that I would not have one sorrow after another." Philippians 2:27

> "Your Love Oh Lord" by Third Day (*Offering: A Worship Album* ©2000, BMG/Brentwood)

Messiah, we worship you. Your mercy never ceases to amaze us. Your faithfulness is unchanging. Your love is so constant, so contagious, and so pure. Keep us faithful to you, Jesus, that we might please you, that we might be more like you, that we might see you on that day. Amen

WEEK 44

■ Psalm 119:121-128
■ 2 Samuel 22:1-25; John 11:1-16

Turn to me and be gracious to me; give your strength to your servant. Psalm 86:16

> "What Kind of Love" by Margaret Becker (*What Kind of Love* ©1999, EMD/Chordant/Sparrow)

Since we are justified by faith, we have peace with God through our Lord Jesus Christ. Romans 5:1

> "All Consuming Fire" by Jennifer Knapp (*Lay It Down* ©2000, EMD/Chordant/Gotee)

O holy God! How do you endure our faithlessness? Our constant sin? Our wanderings? Once again we beg for your mercy and your grace, that relieves our pain! At the foot of the cross, we find our only peace, our only strength. There will we always praise you. Amen

WEEK 44

friday

■ Psalm 119:129-136
■ 2 Samuel 22:26—23:17;
n 11:17-30

many dreams come vanities and a multitude of
ds; but fear God. Ecclesiastes 5:7

"Song of Moses" by Petra (*Petra Praise 2—We
Need Jesus* ©1997, Sony/Word)

wing the fear of God, we try to persuade others;
we ourselves are well known to God.
orinthians 5:11

"My Will" (*Exodus* ©1998, Sony/Word)

Lord, you are so holy, so awesome. You are
ond what our minds can grasp. Guide us each day
e devote our lives to you and become a living
mple of your grace. Amen

WEEK 44

saturday

■ Psalm 119:137-144
■ 2 Samuel 23:18—24:17;
n 11:31-44

ell in the high and holy place, and also with those
are contrite and humble in spirit, to revive the
t of the humble, and to revive the heart of the
rite. Isaiah 57:15

"You Are My All in All" by Dennis Jerrigan (*Vol.
2-You Are My All in All* ©2000, Provident)

ne to me, all you that are weary and are carrying
vy burdens, and I will give you rest.
tthew 11:28

"Hold Me Jesus" by Rich Mullins (*Songs*
©1996, Reunion)

ewing God, you give us strength when we are
k. For this, we give you thanks. Sometimes all we
ly need is for you to hold us, to walk with us, to
de our steps along the journey. Breathe new life
our souls, we pray. Amen

WEEK 45

Watchword for the Week
The King of kings and Lord of lords, who alone has immortality and dwells in unapproachable light, to him be glory and might!
1 Timothy 6:15-16

For you, O God, have tested us; you have tried us as silver is tried. Psalm 66:10

"Awesome God" by Rich Mullins (*Songs* ©1996, Reunion)

For all of us must appear before the judgment seat of Christ; so that each may receive recompense for what has been done in the body. 2 Corinthians 5:10

"Stranger to Holiness" by Steve Camp (*Doing My Best* ©1990, Chordant/Sparrow)

Holy God, we admit there's nothing we can do to earn your love. There is no way we can prove ourselves to you. All you desire is a sincere heart of devotion, a life that's open to your leading. Give us that courage, Lord. Amen

WEEK 45

▬ Psalm 119:145-152
▬ 2 Samuel 24:18-25; 1 Kings 1:1-21; John 11:45-57

The steadfast love of the LORD never ceases. Lamentations 3:22

"I See You" by Rich Mullins (*Songs* ©1996, Reunion)

God has saved us and called us with a holy calling, not according to our works but according to his own purpose and grace. 2 Timothy 1:9

"Never Been Unloved" by Michael W. Smith (*Live the Life* ©1998, Reunion)

Forgiving Savior, our sin makes us stumble each day. Almost despite ourselves you love us and wipe the slate clean. Though we sometimes let you down, we've never been unloved. Thank you, Lord, that your love never fails. Amen

WEEK 45

tuesday

◀ Psalm 119:153-160
◀ 1 Kings 1:22-53; John 12:1-11

LORD God has opened my ear, and I was not
...llious, I did not turn backward. Isaiah 50:5

"Speak to Me" by Rebecca St. James (*God*
©1996, ForeFront)

...anyone who has an ear listen to what the Spirit is
...ng to the churches. To everyone who conquers, I
...give permission to eat from the tree of life that is
...e paradise of God. Revelation 2:7

"Whatever You Ask" by Steve Camp (*Doing My
Best* ©1990, Chordant/Sparrow)

*...er of life, so often you call our names and like
...uel, we seem to miss it. We look to things and
...ple first before looking to you. Forgive us. Give us
...to listen, souls that soften, and feet that move at
...r Spirit's nudging. Amen*

WEEK 45

wednesday

◀ Psalm 119:161-168
◀ 1 Kings 2:1-46; John 12:12-19

...my name's sake I defer my anger, for the sake of
...praise I restrain it for you, so that I may not cut
...off. Isaiah 48:9

"Go and Sin No More" by Rebecca St. James
(*God* ©1996, ForeFront)

...ay, when you hear his voice, do not harden your
...rts. Hebrews 3:15

"Let It Rain" by the Newsboys (*Going Public*
©1994, Star Song)

*...cious God, your forgiveness flows into our souls
...a waterfall. Our sin is washed away with your
...tle touch. Help us to become living examples of
...r forgiveness and grace. Amen*

WEEK 45

- Psalm 119:169-176
- 1 Kings 3:1-28; John 12:20-36

The mighty one, God the LORD, speaks and summons the earth from the rising of the sun to its setting. Psalm 50:1

> "Almighty" by Wayne Watson (*Very Best* ©1995, Word)

Long ago God spoke to our ancestors in many and various ways by the prophets, but in these last days he has spoken to us by a Son. Hebrews 1:1-2

> "Lord I Lift Your Name on High" by Insyderz (*Skalleliua* ©1998, Squint)

Loving Savior, without your grace, we are lost. Without your forgiveness, our souls are in chains, weighted down by sin. Words cannot express the gratitude we feel for our freedom in you. May our hearts beat for you, today and always. Amen

---

WEEK 45

- Psalm 120
- 1 Kings 4:1-28; John 12:37-50

The LORD spoke to Jeremiah: "Now I have put my words in your mouth." Jeremiah 1:9

> "Sing Your Praise to the Lord" by Rich Mullins (*Songs* ©1996, Reunion)

You need endurance, so that when you have done the will of God, you may receive what was promised. Hebrews 10:36

> "Needful Hands" by Jars of Clay (*Exodus* ©1998, Sony/Word)

Lord Jesus, you've given us a voice, through your saving love. Help us to sing praise to you always, no matter what life throws our way. Shine your light upon us and through us. Amen

saturday

Psalm 121

1 Kings 4:29—5:18; John 13:1-17

are my hiding place and my shield; I hope in your
d. Psalm 119:114

"Thy Word" by Amy Grant (*The Collection*
©1990, BMG/RCA)

us said:] "Very truly, I tell you, whoever keeps my
d will never see death." John 8:51

"I Have Decided" by Amy Grant (*The
Collection* ©1990, BMG/RCA)

*, Lord, are our strength. Each day you invite us
 your word and speak to us right where we are.
 us to look for those kernels of truth as we
w you. Amen*

sunday

Watchword for the Week

See, now is the acceptable time;
see, now is the day of salvation.
2 Corinthians 6:2

n though I walk through the darkest valley, I fear no
, for you are with me; your rod and your staff—they
fort me. Psalm 23:4

"We Need Jesus" by Petra (*Petra Praise 2-We
Need Jesus* ©1997, Sony/Word)

comforts us in all our affliction, so that we may be
 to console those who are in any affliction with the
solation with which we ourselves are consoled by
. 2 Corinthians 1:4

"Don't Tell Them Jesus Loves Them"
by Steve Camp (*Doing My Best* ©1990,
Chordant/Sparrow)

*d Jesus, we've been so blessed by your love. As
 love stirs within our souls, we long to pass it on
thers. It's not enough to just share the words. You
 us to meet people where they're at. Equip us to
 love them, as you love us. Amen*

WEEK 46

■■■ Psalm 122
■■■ 1 Kings 6:1-38; John 13:18-30

I will take you for my wife in faithfulness, and you shall know the LORD. Hosea 2:20

> "In This Very Room," (*Fifteen Christian Wedding Favorites* ©1996, Word)

Jesus said: "You will know the truth, and the truth will make you free." John 8:32

> "Freedom" by Code of Ethics (*Code of Ethics* ©1993, ForeFront/Chordant)

We worship you, Lord, for who you are. Your truth sets us free, as you unlock the gates of our hearts. A part of you lives within us, guiding us to your truth each day. Guide us Lord, we pray. Amen

WEEK 46

■■■ Psalm 123
■■■ 1 Kings 7:1-33; John 13:31-38

I love you, O LORD, my strength. Psalm 18:1

> "Out of My Hands" by Tony Vincent (*Tony Vincent* ©1995. For more information click on www.tonyvincent.com)

Be strong in the Lord, and in the strength of his power. Ephesians 6:10

> "Show Your Power" by Petra (*Petra Praise 2- We Need Jesus* ©1997, Sony/Word)

Lord, we try so hard to make it on our own. And how humbling it is to realize that our lives, the things we worry about so much, are out of our hands. Help us to surrender our concerns at your feet daily. You are our strength. Amen

wednesday

Psalm 124
1 Kings 7:34—8:16; John 14:1-14

now that I, even I, am he; there is no god beside
Deuteronomy 32:39

"Be Still" by the Newsboys (*Going Public*
©1994, EMD/Sparrow/Star Song)

us said: "And this is eternal life, that they may
w you, the only true God, and Jesus Christ whom
have sent." John 17:3

"Where You Belong/Turn Your Eyes upon Jesus"
by the Newsboys (*Not Ashamed* ©1992, Star
Song)

d, the things of earth just fade away when we
k at you. You are the chief elder of our hearts,
w and always. Help us to just be still and know
t you are God. Amen

thursday

Psalm 125
1 Kings 8:17-53; John 14:15-24

he stands at the right hand of the needy, to save
m from those who would condemn them to death.
lm 109:31

"One Deed" by Tony Vincent (*One Deed*
©1997, Star Song)

us said: "Blessed are the poor; for theirs is the
gdom of God." Luke 6:20

"Reach Out" by Tony Vincent (*One Deed*
©1997, Star Song)

cious God, everything we have is a gift from you.
re are so many hurting people who don't know
. Help us to reach out beyond ourselves, beyond
friends, beyond people who are just like us, to
re your healing grace with others. Amen

WEEK 46

▆▆▆ Psalm 126
▆▆▆ 1 Kings 8:54—9:19;
John 14:25—15:7

Remember the long way that the LORD your God has led you these forty years in the wilderness, in order to humble you, testing you to know what was in your heart. Deuteronomy 8:2

> "Psalm 139" by Rebecca St. James (*God* ©1996, ForeFront)

For the man on whom this sign of healing had been performed was more than forty years old. Acts 4:22

> "All Things Are Possible" (*WoW Worship Green* ©2001, Sony/Epic)

You search us and you know us, loving Lord. There's nothing in our lives that we could possibly hide from you. You see the good things and what we try to sweep under a rug within our souls, too. Clear out the cobwebs in our souls and know our hearts today. Amen

WEEK 46

▆▆▆ Psalm 127
▆▆▆ 1 Kings 9:20—10:29; John 15:8-17

In your steadfast love you have led the people whom you redeemed. Exodus 15:13

> "Marks of the Cross" by Petra (*Wake-Up Call* ©1993, Word)

Live in love, as Christ loved us. Ephesians 5:2

> "Love One Another" by Michael W. Smith (*Change Your World* ©1992, Reunion)

You call us to be daring as we share your love each day. Lord, we know deep down your love is the only way hardened hearts are softened and bound up souls are given freedom and release. Help us to walk the talk, to truly love one another. Amen

sunday

Watchword for the Week

We must all appear before the judgment seat of Christ.
2 Corinthians 5:10

...o have I in heaven but you? And there is nothing ...earth that I desire other than you. Psalm 73:25

..."Redeemer" by Nicole C. Mullen (*Nicole C. Mullen* ©2000, Sony/Word)

...us said:] "If you know me, you will know my ...er also." John 14:7

..."Ancient of Days" (*WoW Worship—Today's 30 Most Powerful Worship Songs* ©1999, Sony/Word)

...ious Father, you demand our stillness so that our ...ts might be prepared for your work. We know that ...v in you do we deserve righteousness. By your hand ...e we are brought out of darkness into light. May ...r shield be our only armor. Your faithfulness is like ...ighty mountain and you will not be moved. Amen

monday

Psalm 128
1 Kings 11:1-25; John 15:18—16:4

... LORD your God knows your going through this ...t wilderness. Deuteronomy 2:7

..."I'm Trading My Sorrows" (*WoW Worship Green* ©2001, Sony/Epic)

...en Jesus saw the crowds, he had compassion for ...m, because they were harassed and helpless; like a ...ep without a shepherd. Matthew 9:36

..."Healing" by Bebo Norman (*Ten Thousand Days* ©1999, Sony/Word)

...cious Lord, because of your death on the cross we ...no longer chained to this world. Instead, you have ...pted us to live in your Spirit. Money, cars, ...demics, and relationships are no longer idols in ...lives if we live in your Spirit. When our hearts ... away, we humbly ask you to draw us near once ...n. Amen

WEEK 47

tuesday

Psalm 129
1 Kings 11:26—12:24; John 16:5-16

For surely, I know the plans I have for you, says the
LORD, plans for your welfare and not for harm, to give
you a future with hope. Jeremiah 29:11

> "All Things Are Possible" (*WoW Worship Green*
> ©2001, Sony/Epic)

God's love was revealed among us in this way; God
sent his only Son into the world so that we might live
through him. 1 John 4:9

> "We Fall Down" (*WoW Worship Green* ©2001,
> Sony/Epic)

*Eternal Savior, you are our stronghold and we want to
rest in your embrace. We know you have not promised us ill will, but instead you want to give us the
desires of our hearts. We want to fall more in love
with you and desire you above all else. For you are
the only one that truly satisfies our every yearning.
Amen*

WEEK 47

wednesday

Psalm 130
1 Kings 12:25—13:19; John 16:17-33

Boaz spoke to the cutters: "The LORD be with you!"
They answered: "The LORD bless you!" Ruth 2:4

> "The Hammer Holds" by Bebo Norman (*Ten
> Thousand Days* ©1999, BMG/Brentwood)

The point is this: The one who sows sparingly will also
reap sparingly, and the one who sows bountifully will
also reap bountifully. 2 Corinthians 9:6

> "How Long Will Be Too Long" by Michael W.
> Smith (*Go West Young Man* ©1990, Reunion)

*King of all creation, help us to use the gifts we have
been granted to edify your kingdom. May we rejoice
as your family grows. Encourage our hearts to be slow
to anger and quick to love. We want to adorn our
lives with your beauty and glory. Amen*

WEEK 47

Psalm 131
1 Kings 13:20—14:20; John 17:1-19

For your name's sake, O LORD, pardon my guilt, for it is great. Psalm 25:11

"Amazing Grace" by Gospel Gangstaz (*I Can See Clearly Now* ©1999, Provident)

Be kind to one another, tenderhearted, forgiving one another, as God in Christ has forgiven you. Ephesians 4:32

"Between You and Me" dc Talk (*WoW 1997* ©1996, EMD/Chordant)

Holy Father, help us to be imitators of your truth. Help us to cleanse our lives by humbly asking forgiveness in your name. May we remember everything we are and have come to be is by your hand. We thank you for bringing us from death to life although we were undeserving. Amen

WEEK 47

Psalm 132
1 Kings 14:21—15:8; John 17:20-26

Far be it from us that we should rebel against the LORD, and turn away this day from following the LORD. Joshua 22:29

"Into Jesus" by dc Talk (*WoW 1999* ©1998, EMD/Chordant)

It is required of stewards that they be found trustworthy. 1 Corinthians 4:2

"Stand" by Bebo Norman (*Ten Thousand Days* ©1999, BMG/Brentwood)

Gracious Father, may we remember always that your grace is patient and your love is kind. May we be patient with your ways and your desires for our lives. Help us remember that you are love and we are only able to love ourselves and others through you. Amen .

WEEK 47

■■■ Psalm 133
■■■ 1 Kings 15:9—16:14; John 18:1-11

I will praise the LORD's word. Psalm 56:10

> "We Fall Down" (*WoW Worship Green* ©2001, Sony/Epic)

[Paul wrote:] "We will not boast beyond limits, but will keep within the field that God has assigned to us." 2 Corinthians 10:13

> "Faithful to Me—Prelude" by Jennifer Knapp (*Kansas* ©1998, EMD/Chordant)

Abba, Father, we cry out knowing that you chose us before we ever chose you. We praise you for the truth you give us in your word. We pray today for humility so that our hearts may be resigned only to your will. We know that when we decrease you increase in our lives. Amen

WEEK 48

Watchword for the Week
Be dressed for action and have your lamps lit. Luke 12:35

I gave them my statutes and showed them my ordinances, by whose observance everyone shall live. Ezekiel 20:11

> "Thy Word" by Amy Grant (*Collection* ©1990, Myrrh)

Jesus spoke to Martha: "I am the resurrection and the life. Those who believe in me, even though they die, they shall live." John 11:25

> "More Than You'll Ever Know" by Watermark (*All Things New* ©2000, Sony/Word)

Most gracious Lord, we thank you for being our saving grace and for always providing for us even when we do not deserve your love. May our lives be a living sacrifice to you where we entrust that to die is truly to gain life everlasting. Amen

monday

■ Psalm 134
■ 1 Kings 16:15—17:24; John 18:12-24

t your burden on the LORD, and he will sustain
. Psalm 55:22

"One More Broken Heart" by Point of Grace
(*Point of Grace* ©1993, Word)

cares of the world, the lure of wealth, and the
re for other things come in and choke the word,
it yields nothing. Mark 4:19

"Romans" by Jennifer Knapp (*Kansas* ©1998,
EMD/Chordant)

er God, we are rich men and women only when
give our whole lives to you. Because we are no
er part of this world we gain nothing from it by
g in the flesh. We pray for heavenly riches of
 love and compassion to rain down upon our
s. May we be satisfied in you alone. Amen

tuesday

■ Psalm 135:1-12
■ 1 Kings 18:1-45; John 18:25-40

nd your ways and your doings, and let me dwell
you in this place. Jeremiah 7:3

"Refine Me" by Jennifer Knapp (*Kansas* ©1998,
EMD/Chordant)

fruits worthy of repentance. Luke 3:8

"Today" by Waterdeep (*Enter the Worship
Circle* ©Waterdeep. For more information click
on www.waterdeep.com)

 we come to you with all of our burdens and
dly sins. We ask that they might be replaced
anently in exchange for you. We repent for all
misgivings and unworthy thoughts. You alone are
hy. Amen

WEEK 48

■■ **Psalm 135:13-21**
■■ **1 Kings 19:1-21; John 19:1-11**

The LORD our God has shown us his glory and greatness. Deuteronomy 3:24

> "I Want to Know You" by Sonicflood (*Sonicflood* ©1999, EMD/Chordant)

Those who love me, will be loved by my Father, and I will love them and reveal myself to them. John 14:21

> "Knowing You" by the Passion Band (*Better Is One Day* ©2000, EMD/Sparrow)

Sweet Lord, you are so eager to reveal to us your glory. Open our eyes to your love. Only in the realms of our hearts can this change begin to take place because that is your domain. We ask you to come home into our hearts that we may desire you more and more every day, knowing your unconditional love for us. Amen

WEEK 48

■■ **Psalm 136**
■■ **1 Kings 20:1-21; John 19:12-24**

All your works shall give thanks to you, O LORD, and all your faithful shall bless you. Psalm 145:10

> "Lord You Have My Heart" by Delirious? (*Cutting Edge* ©1997, EMD/Sparrow)

We give you thanks, Lord God Almighty, who are and who were, for you have taken your great power and begun to reign. Revelation 11:17

> "Jesus, Lover of My Soul" by Hillsongs (*Shout to Lord-Platinum Collection* ©2000, Sony/Word)

Father Most High, we want to know you so much more. We pray for your Spirit to consume our entire beings. We praise you for everything you have done in the past, everything you have done today, and everything that you have promised you will do. We rest in knowing that your hand is always at work. Amen

friday

Psalm 137
1 Kings 20:22—21:16; John 19:25-37

...r name, O God, like your praise reaches to the ...ls of the earth. Psalm 48:10

"The Man Inside" by Bebo Norman (*Ten Thousand Days* ©1999, BMG/Brentwood)

...rist said:] "This good news of the kingdom will be ...claimed throughout the world, as a testimony to all nations." Matthew 24:14

"When You Believe" by Whitney Houston and Mariah Carey (*When You Believe: The Prince of Egypt* ©1999)

...d God, remind us constantly that you are always ...re. We know that by saying your precious name ... become invincible to the pains of this world and ... fearful of nothing. We pray that our lips might be ...pired to preach your love to all the nations. Amen

saturday

Psalm 138:1-5
1 Kings 21:17—22:28;
...n 19:38—20:9

...ld my life in my hand continually, but I do not ...et your law. Psalm 119:109

"His Grace Is Sufficient" by Jennifer Knapp (*Kansas* ©1998, EMD/Chordant)

...the love of God is this, that we obey his ...mandments. 1 John 5:3

"Light the Fire" by Liam Lawton (*Light the Fire* ©2000, GIA)

...d of stillness, in such a busy and chaotic world we ...v that our hearts may turn inward to the com-...dments that you have intimately written on our ...rts. We are reminded that even when we did not ...erve forgiveness you loved us so much that you ...e your only Son to pay the debt. Amen

WEEK 49

Watchword for the Week
Lo, your king comes to you,
triumphant and victorious is he.
Zechariah 9:9

Yet God my King is from of old, working salvation in
the earth. Psalm 74:12

> "Heart of Worship" by Sonicflood with the
> Passion Worship Band (*Road to One Day* ©1999,
> EMD/Sparrow)

The crowds that went ahead of him and that followed
him were shouting, "Hosanna to the Son of David!
Blessed is the one who comes in the name of the
Lord." Matthew 21:9

> "Hiding Place" by Steven Curtis Chapman (*Best
> of Steven Curtis Chapman* ©2000, Madacy
> Entertainment Group)

*God of everything, you are truly ancient of days and
you will rule until the end of time. You have already
gone before us to clear the path to righteousness. We
praise your unrelenting faithfulness to us. Help us to
be imitators of your ways. Amen*

WEEK 49

■ Psalm 138:6-8
■ 1 Kings 22:29-53; John 20:10-23

Then you shall know that I am the LORD your God.
Exodus 16:12

> "Holiness" by Sonicflood (*Sonicflood* ©1999,
> EMD/Chordant)

Jesus said to them, "If God were your Father, you
would love me; for I came from God and now I am
here. I did not come on my own, but he sent me."
John 8:42

> "Let Everything That Has Breath" by Passion
> Worship Band (*Better Is One Day* ©2000,
> EMD/Sparrow)

*Precious Maker, even when we turn away from you,
scorn you, and deny you, your love is relentless. Lord,
help us to realize that only when we replace the idols
of this world with you can we truly know your love.
Teach us to recklessly abandon ourselves to you and
lead our lives with your all-powerful wisdom. Amen*

tuesday

Psalm 139:1-6

2 Kings 1:1—2:18; John 20:24-31

...any shall be purified, cleansed and refined.
...aniel 12:10

"I Could Sing of Your Love Forever" by Delirious? (*Cutting Edge* ©1997, EMD/Sparrow)

...e faith that you have, have as your own conviction
...fore God. Blessed are those who have no reason to
...ndemn themselves because of what they approve.
...mans 14:22

"Better Is One Day" by Passion Worship Band
(*Better Is One Day* ©2000, EMD/Sparrow)

...d, we come to you with hearts that are
...wntrodden and heavy laden with sin. You send us
...ay with hearts full of joy and compassion. You are
...e Lord of the dance and you set our feet to
...ncing. Thank you. Teach us to forgive, love, and
...ow mercy as you so freely and lovingly do for us.
...men

wednesday

Psalm 139:7-12

2 Kings 2:19—3:27; John 21:1-14

...ppy are those to whom the LORD imputes no iniqui-
...and in whose spirit there is no deceit. Psalm 32:2

"Agnus Dei" by Passion Worship Band (*Better Is
One Day* ©2000, EMD/Sparrow)

...ou do not forgive others, neither will your Father
...give your trespasses. Matthew 6:15

"To Speak Your Name" by Passion Worship
Band (*Better Is One Day* ©2000, EMD/Sparrow)

...d, because you have blessed us with your life we
...ire to be holy and blameless in your sight. Help us
...walk in your ways and make others disciples of the
...h. You are truly holy and without you we would
...beggars with no home to return to. Thank you for
...paring us a home in heaven. Amen

WEEK 49

■■■ Psalm 139:13-16
■■■ 2 Kings 4:1-37; John 21:15—21:25; Acts 1:1-5

Out of my distress I called on the LORD; the LORD answered me and set me in a broad place.
Psalm 118:5

> "Trading my Sorrows" (*I Could Sing of Your Love Vol. 1* ©2000, EMD/Chordant)

You did not receive a spirit of slavery to fall back into fear, but you have received a spirit of adoption, through which we cry "Abba, Father." Romans 8:15

> "Shout to the North" by Passion Worship Band (*Road to One Day* ©2000, EMD/Sparrow)

Father, come fall on us and dress us in your wisdom and guidance. In the struggles and sorrows of life you have come that we might have life—life to the fullest. Help us to remember that life outside of you is death. You have adopted us as your children and we can rest peacefully in your arms in eternity. Amen

WEEK 49

■■■ Psalm 139:17-24
■■■ 2 Kings 4:38—5:14; Acts 1:6-19

Wash your heart clean of wickedness so that you may be saved. How long shall your evil schemes lodge within you? Jeremiah 4:14

> "One Pure and Holy Passion" by Passion Worship Band (*Oneday Live* ©1999, EMD/Sparrow)

Rid yourselves of all sordidness and rank growth of wickedness, and welcome with meekness the implanted word that has the power to save your souls. James 1:21

> "Hands and Feet" by Audio Adrenaline (*Hit Parade* ©2001, EMD/Chordant)

Father, we pray today that you will create in us "a new creation." Wash us with your blood and reveal to us the way to righteousness. Without you we are lost, but in you we find ourselves and our future. Thank you for accepting us just as we are and meeting us just where we are. We praise you for your awesome works. Amen

WEEK 49

■ Psalm 140:1-5
■ 2 Kings 5:15—6:19; Acts 1:20—2:4

people have committed two evils: They have
aken me, the fountain of living water, and dug out
erns for themselves, cracked cisterns that can hold
water. Jeremiah 2:13

"Walk Down This Mountain" by Bebo Norman
(*Ten Thousand Days* ©1999, Provident)

us said to her, "Everyone who drinks of this water
be thirsty again." John 4:13

"Hanging by a Moment" by Lifehouse (*No
Name Face* ©2000, UNI/Dream Works)

ster of the universe, you know more than we
'd ever imagine. The more we strive to know
ut you, the less we realize we know. But the one
 thing is that you hear us when we pray and you
ond according to what is best for us. Father, if
 must, bring us to a point of brokenness so that
might know your power and grace all the more
 share it with all the nations. For you are the
re of all nations! Amen

WEEK 50

sunday

Watchword for the Week
Stand up and raise your heads, for
your redemption is drawing near.
Luke 21:28

 me, O LORD, my God! Save me according to your
dfast love. Psalm 109:26

"Here With Me" by Plumb
(*Candycoatedwaterdrops* ©1999,
BMG/Brentwood)

r answered him, "Lord, if it is you, command me
ome to you on the water." He said, "Come."
thew 14:28-29

"Walk on Water" by Audio Adrenaline (*Bloom*
©1996, EMD/Chordant)

er, we know there is nothing we can do without
 Please give us the strength and the courage to
le the big plans you have for us. Help us to listen
our words so we know what it is you want us to
Amen

WEEK 50

■ Psalm 140:6-13
■ 2 Kings 6:20—7:20; Acts 2:5-13

David strengthened himself in the LORD his God.
1 Samuel 30:6

> "Right Place" by Petra (*No Doubt* ©1995, Sony/Word)

The apostles said to the Lord, "Increase our faith!"
Luke 17:5

> "Shifting Sand" by Caedmon's Call (*40 Acres* ©1999, BMG/Brentwood)

Heavenly Father, there are so many things that come at us in everyday life that try to make us waver in our walk with you. We pray you will give us faith that is unmovable. Help us to say no to the things that make us stumble. Amen

WEEK 50

■ Psalm 141:1-4
■ 2 Kings 8:1-29; Acts 2:14-30

Happy are all who take refuge in him. Psalm 2:11

> "Hanging by a Moment" by Lifehouse (*No Name Face* ©2000, UNI/Dream Works)

Do not, therefore, abandon that confidence of yours; it brings a great reward. Hebrews 10:35

> "Karaoke Superstars" by Superchic[k] (*Karaoke Superstars* ©2001, Chordant)

Heavenly Father, with your help, we know we can do anything. You have freed us from being timid and shy. With you we can be bold and self-assured. When we do feel afraid, we thank you that you are there for us. We can come running to you and you give us strength. We can be joyful even in times of trial as long as we turn to you. Amen

wednesday

Psalm 141:5-10
2 Kings 9:1-37; Acts 2:31-47

LORD sent me to proclaim liberty to the captives.
ah 61:1

"Free" by Ginny Owens (*Without Condition*
©1999, Rocketown)

hember those who are in prison, as though you
e in prison with them. Hebrews 13:3

"Got You on My Mind" by Eric Clapton (*Reptile*
©2001, WEA/Warner)

d, you have rescued us from our life of sin! Thank
for freeing us so we no longer have to know fear.
pray for those who have physical chains around
n for speaking your word. Comfort them. May
be a light to those around them. Amen

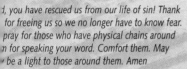

---

thursday

Psalm 142
2 Kings 10:1-36; Acts 3:1-10

our days I will speak the word and fulfill it, says
LORD God. Ezekiel 12:25

"Are You Ready?" by Creed (*Human Clay*
©1999, BMG/Wind Up)

even boast in God through our Lord Jesus Christ,
ugh whom we have now received reconciliation.
nans 5:11

"Anything" by PFR (*Them* ©1996,
Sparrow/Chordant)

d, you have told us to be ready for your return.
't let us fall asleep in our relationship with you.
e us the boldness to tell others about your return.
e us the boldness to tell others about the wonder-
things you've done in our lives. Let us be a living
imony of your greatness. Amen

WEEK 50

▬▬ Psalm 143:1-6
▬▬ 2 Kings 11:1-21; Acts 3:11-23

I will set my eyes upon them for good, and I will bring them back to this land. I will build them up, and not tear them down; I will plant them, and not pluck them up. Jeremiah 24:6

> "Imagine Me without You" by Jaci Velasquez (*Crystal Clear* ©2000, Sony/Word)

The one who was seated on the throne said, "See, I am making all things new." Revelation 21:5

> "Not Going Back" by Eli (*Second Hand Clothing* ©1999, EMD/Chordant)

Don't let us look back to our sinful days, Father. Don't let us get caught up in the earthly activities those around us are in. Let us look to you and your holiness. Keep our thoughts holy and pure. Guide our actions so they reflect you. Amen

WEEK 50

▬▬ Psalm 143:7-12
▬▬ 2 Kings 12:1—13:25; Acts 3:24—4:11

So when the woman saw that the tree was good for food, and that it was a delight to the eyes, and that the tree was to be desired to make one wise, she took of its fruit and ate; and she also gave some to her husband, who was with her, and he ate. Genesis 3:6

> "Trampoline" by Miss Angie (*One Hundred Million Eyeballs* ©1997, Word)

For if the many died through the one man's trespass, much more surely have the grace of God and the free gift in the grace of the one man, Jesus Christ, abounded for the many. Romans 5:15

> "Saviour of My Universe" by All Star United (*All Star United* ©1997, Provident)

Because of one man's sin (Adam) we are in a world of sinners. Because of one man's obedience (Jesus) we are made righteous. Thank you, Father, for sending your Son so we could live. Don't let us lose sight of Jesus. He is truly the greatest gift! Amen

sunday

Watchword for the Week

Prepare the way of the LORD; the LORD God comes with might.
Isaiah 40:3, 10

...u say, "The way of the LORD is unfair." Hear now, O ...use of Israel: Is my way unfair? Is it not your ways ...t are unfair? Ezekiel 18:25

"Wake Up Call" by Relient K (*Relient K* ©2000, EMD/Chordant)

...here injustice on God's part? By no means! For he ...s to Moses, "I will have mercy on whom I have ...cy, and I will have compassion on whom I have ...npassion." Romans 9:14-15

"Unforgetful You" by Jars of Clay (*If I Left the Zoo* ©1999, Provident)

...avenly Father, we don't always understand why bad ...gs happen. Remind us you are always in control. ...matter what happens, let us praise your name. ...er let us doubt your love for us. Times can be ...icult and trying. Let us keep our eyes set on you so ...don't stray. Amen

---

monday

Psalm 144:1-4
2 Kings 14:1-29; Acts 4:12-22

...the LORD our God belong mercy and forgiveness.
...iel 9:9

"Let Mercy Lead" by Rich Mullins (*Songs* ©1996, Reunion)

...hich of these three, do you think, was a neighbor ...ne man who fell into the hands of the robbers?" ...said, "The one who showed him mercy." Jesus ...l to him, "Go and do likewise." Luke 10:36-37

"Mercy Came Running" by Phillips, Craig, and Dean (*Favorite Songs of All* ©1998, EMD/Chordant)

...give us, Lord, for not treating others the way you ...t us to. Help us to put aside our selfish desires so ...can focus on showing your love to others. Make ...concern to be for others, not for ourselves. Let us ...like you. Amen

WEEK 51

■ Psalm 144:5-8
■ 2 Kings 15:1-38; Acts 4:23-37

Which of you desires life, and covets many days to enjoy good? Keep your tongue from evil, and your lips from speaking deceit. Psalm 34:12-13

"Nothing at All" by Third Day (*Third Day* ©1996, Reunion)

There is nothing outside a person that by going in can defile, but the things that come out are what defile. Mark 7:15

"Just Between You and Me" by dc Talk (*Jesus Freak* ©1995, EMD/Chordant)

There are things that come from our mouths and minds that are not pleasing to you, Lord. Make our mouths speak only encouragement to our friends, family and neighbors. Make our thoughts holy and pure. Make our actions testimonies of your wonderful works. Let others see you by the way we act. Amen

---

WEEK 51

■ Psalm 144:9-15
■ 2 Kings 16:1—17:6; Acts 5:1-11

Ah, you who acquit the guilty for a bribe, and deprive the innocent of their rights! Isaiah 5:22-23

"Hands" by Jewel (*Spirit* ©1998, WEA/Atlantic)

For with the judgment you make you will be judged, and the measure you give will be the measure you get. Matthew 7:2

"Into You" by Jennifer Knapp (*Lay It Down* ©2000, EMD/Chordant)

We know there are people who don't feel loved. Let us show them your love through the talents you have given us. We want to use the gifts you have given us to help others. Place us in situations where our gifts are needed. Amen

thursday

◀ Psalm 145:1-7
◀ 2 Kings 17:7-41; Acts 5:12-16

LORD makes the blind see. Psalm 146:8

"Written on My Heart" by Plus One (*Promise* ©2000, WEA/Atlantic)

us spoke to Bartimaeus:] "Go, your faith has made well." Immediately he regained his sight and fol- ed him on the way. Mark 10:52

"Beautiful Day" by U2 (*All That You Can't Leave Behind* ©2000, UNI/Interscope)

, we pray that you will reach out and lay your d on us. We pray also that you will lead us to the e you can best use us and that we will follow out question. Show us that we don't need to see re we're going because you are in control. ough faith, we know you will take care of us. ough faith, we will follow you. Amen

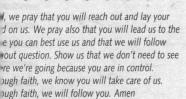

friday

◀ Psalm 145:8-16
◀ 2 Kings 18:1-37; Acts 5:17-41

I am with you, says the LORD, to save you. miah 30:11

"There You Are" by Carolyn Arends (*Feel Free* ©1997, Reunion)

prayer of faith will save the sick, and the Lord will them up. James 5:15

"Melodies from Heaven" by Kirk Franklin (*Watcha Lookin' 4* ©1995, UNI/Gospocentric)

want to thank you, Lord, for always being with When we're healthy or sick, on our way to work, ool, the movies, or to church, you're with us. How forting to know you never leave us. We know we be anywhere, pray, and you'll hear us. Thank you always hearing our prayers. Amen

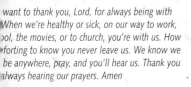

WEEK 51

■ Psalm 145:17-21
■ 2 Kings 19:1-28; Acts 5:42—6:7

He has told you, O mortal, what is good; and what does the LORD require of you, but to do justice, and to love kindness, and to walk humbly with your God. Micah 6:8

> "True Believers" by Phil Keaggy (*True Believers* ©1995, Sparrow Songs/Chordant Music/BMI)

In everything do to others as you would have them do to you. Matthew 7:12

> "Rumor Weed" by The W's (*WoW 2000* ©1999, EMD/Chordant)

Father, let us consider our actions before we do them. Help us evaluate whether our deeds will be pleasing to you. Forgive us when we refuse to listen to you and we hurt those around us. Thank you for your forgiveness. Thank you for the forgiveness others have shown us. We pray we can forgive like you. Amen

WEEK 52

Watchword for the Week

Rejoice in the Lord always; again I will say, Rejoice. Let your gentleness be known to everyone. The Lord is near. Philippians 4:4-5

For a brief moment I abandoned you, but with great compassion I will gather you. Isaiah 54:7

> "Cry for Love" by Michael W. Smith (*I'll Lead You Home* ©1995, Reunion)

And when he comes home, he calls together his friends and neighbors, saying to them, "Rejoice with me, for I have found my sheep that was lost." Luke 15:6

> "Everytime You Say Goodbye" by Alison Krauss (*Everytime You Say Goodbye* ©1992, UNI/Rounder)

Lord, there are times we don't want to do what you want us to. We become rebellious children. Even though we stray from the fold, we know we are never beyond your reach. Thank you that every time we stray, you welcome us back. Thank you for your unfailing love. Amen

Psalm 146
2 Kings 19:29—20:21; Acts 6:8—7:5

n the heavens you uttered judgment; the earth
ed and was still when God rose up to establish
ment, to save all the oppressed of the earth.
m 76:8-9

"Gravity" by Out Of the Grey (*Gravity* ©1995,
Sparrow Song/BMI)

ry said:] "My spirit rejoices in God my Savior, for
as looked with favor on the lowliness of his
ant. Surely, from now on all generations will call
blessed." Luke 1:47-48

"Mary, Did You Know?" by Mark Lowry (*Mark
Lowry on Broadway* ©2001, EMD/Chordant)

venly Father, you sent your Son to earth for our
What an incredible gift! We know one day Jesus
return and save us physically from this world.
l then, may we be ready. May our days be filled
praises of your name. Amen

Psalm 147:1-6
2 Kings 21:1—22:10; Acts 7:6-16

let people ride over our heads; we went through
and through water; yet you have brought us out
spacious place. Psalm 66:12

"Christmas Lullaby (I'll Lead You Home)" by
Amy Grant (*Christmas to Remember* ©1999,
Myrrh/A&M)

angel said to the shepherds: "Do not be afraid;
ee—I am bringing you good news of great joy for
he people; to you is born this day in the city of
id a Savior, who is the Messiah." Luke 2:10-11

"Hark! The Herald Angels Sing" by Take 6 (*He
Is Christmas* ©1999, WEA/Warner Brothers)

, let us take time out to truly thank you for the
of your Son. That is yet another example of how
h you love us. You sacrificed your only Son so we
d be with you forever. Help us remember that.
en

WEEK 52

■ Psalm 147:7-14
■ 2 Kings 22:11—23:30; Acts 7:17-29

The LORD judges the peoples. Psalm 7:8

> "I Surrender All" by the Newsboys (*Love Liberty Disco* ©1999, EMD/Sparrow)

And this is the judgment; that the light has come into the world. John 3:19

> "Love Has Come" by Amy Grant (*Christmas Album* ©1983, Myrrh/Word)

You sent your Son so the world would know what love was. Though we fall short of your perfect example, you still love us. Thank you for loving us, not because we've done wonderful things, but because you've done wonderful things. Your love is truly perfect. Amen

WEEK 52

■ Psalm 147:15-20
■ 2 Kings 23:31—24:20; Acts 7:30-44

I will save them from all the apostasies into which they have fallen, and will cleanse them. Then they shall be my people. Ezekiel 37:23

> "Lord of the Dance" by Steven Curtis Chapman (*Signs of Life* ©1996, Sparrow)

Simeon said: "For my eyes have seen your salvation, which you have prepared in the presence of all peoples." Luke 2:30-31

> "Under the Influence" by Anointed (*Under the Influence* ©1996, Sony/Word)

Holy Father, we thank you that you are our leader. We don't have to wonder aimlessly in this world because we know you will show us the way. You will guide us. We know when we fall you will pick us up. We know you will protect us. Lead the way, Lord. We will follow. Amen

friday

Psalm 148:1-6
2 Kings 25:1-30; Acts 7:45-60

where are your gods that you made for yourself?
hem come, if they can save you, in your time of
ble. Jeremiah 2:28

"Bully Go Home" by The W's (*Trouble with X*
©1999, EMD/Five Minute Walk)

Peter said to him, "May your silver perish with
because you thought you could obtain God's gift
money! You have no part or share in this, for
heart is not right before God." Acts 8:20-21

"More Than Gold" by Geoff Moore and the
Distance (*Greatest Hits* ©1996, EMD/Chordant)

know there is nothing on earth that can eternally
us. Only through your Son are we saved. Help
put aside the things of this world that consume
ime we should be spending with you. We want
as our priority. Amen

saturday

Psalm 148:7-14
1 Chronicles 1:1-37; Acts 8:1-8

care, or you will be seduced into turning away,
ng other gods and worshiping them.
teronomy 11:16

"And Your Bird Can Sing" by The Beatles
(*Revolver* ©1966, EMD/Capitol)

ot let your hearts be troubled. Believe in God,
ve also in me. John 14:1

"More to This" by Third Day (*Conspiracy #5*
©1997, Reunion/Provident)

er, we get so caught up in material things that we
t about placing you first in our lives. We put
s such as our friends or our appearance in your
. Lord, take those things out of our lives! We
you to be first. Fill us with your love and desires
e don't want those things anymore. Let us
ad crave you. Amen

writer's bios

[Ch]istell Benson is a sophomore at Luther College in [De]corah, Iowa. She is currently double majoring in [hi]story and anthropology. She lives the other three [m]onths of the year in Chaska, Minn., where she [lo]ves to read and go to movies. She also enjoys [wri]ting and riding horses.

[M]ary Bielke lives in Ephraim, Wis., where she serves [as] pastor of the Ephraim Moravian Church. She is a [gr]aduate of the University of Wisconsin-Whitewater [an]d Moravian Theological Seminary. She enjoys [wr]iting, playing tennis, music, and traveling.

[Ra]chel Bruckart lives in Emmaus, Pa. She attends [Em]maus High School and will be a junior during the [20]01-2002 school year. She is very active in her [ch]urch youth groups and choirs. In a few years she [pl]ans on attending Moravian College and majoring in [eit]her music or psychology.

[Gl]enn E. Carolan's habitat is in Catasauqua, Pa., with [hi]s cat Ebenezer. A computer network engineer, he [w]as previously involved as a youth leader/guitarist/ [m]usician for 15 years. Glenn loves to help facilitate [w]orship with his church praise team, his band [Th]eWord, and any other ways. Any spare time is [sp]ent sleeping or Jeepin'. Future plans: to spend [m]ore time with God!

[An]drew Davison is currently a senior at Lake Mills [(W]is.) High School. He is a member of the Lake Mills [M]oravian Church and the treasurer of the Western [R]egional Youth Council. In his spare time he enjoys [w]hitewater kayaking, soccer, and hanging out with [fri]ends. He hopes to attend St. Lawrence University [in] Canton, N.Y., in the fall of 2002.

[M]ichael Forrest is the pastor of youth and young [ad]ults at Ebenezer Bible Fellowship Church, in [Be]thlehem, Pa. He received a B.S. in business [ad]ministration from The Master's College and is [cu]rrently working on an M.A. in biblical studies at [Tri]nity Theological Seminary. His favorite things to do [in]clude playing the guitar, leading worship, playing [ul]timate Frisbee and reading, especially John Piper [bo]oks.

David Furst lives in Ham Lake, Minn. A senior at the Pact Charter School in Coon Rapids, he plans on attending Bethel College to major in journalism. He is now playing in a new and upcoming band called Overpass. Their CD was released in August 2001. He enjoys singing and playing bass guitar.

Jason Graf is a second-year seminary student at Moravian Theological Seminary. He plans on graduating with a master of divinity degree in May 2003. Music is one of his great loves in life, along with God and his wife. Originally from Lake Mills, Wis., Jason calls the Midwest his home while he and his wife, Heidi, currently live in Bethlehem, Pa.

Jennifer Guarino is a junior at Elon University in Elon, N.C. She is a journalism major and hopes to pursue a career in print media or public relations. She is the managing editor of *The Pendulum*, Elon's student-run newspaper. In her free time, Jennifer likes to work on her scrapbooks, read, and spend time with friends. She is a member of Unity Moravian Church in Lewisville, N.C.

Melissa Hertzog is a native of Nazareth, Pa., and a 2001 graduate from Moravian Theological Seminary, Bethlehem, Pa. She was recently installed as part of the pastoral staff of the New Dorp Moravian Church in Staten Island, N.Y. Missy loves music and has shared her talents in the areas of voice and piano with the church for many years.

Carissa Holton is a native of Minnesota and currently lives in Iowa with her husband and son. She enjoys running, cooking, writing stories, and sharing Christ with other people.

Jenn Johnson lives in Maple Grove, Minn., and serves as the youth/Christian education director at Christ's Community Church. She graduated from Gustavus Adolphus College, St. Peter, Minn., in 1999 with an English major and a music minor. She enjoys writing, literature, family time, and singing.

Vicki Johnson lives in Bethlehem Pa. A senior at Kutztown University of Pennsylvania, she plans to graduate with a B.F.A. in related arts in the spring of 2002. In addition to her studies in writing, literature, and dance, she enjoys all types of music. For the past three years she has also coached junior high cheerleading at Bethlehem Christian School.

Kerry Krauss has been serving as pastor of the Edgeboro Moravian Church for $3\frac{1}{2}$ years. He and his wife, Karen, recently celebrated the birth of their first son, Jackson Isaiah, whom they describe as "a great and tremendous blessing for us." Kerry is very involved with outdoor youth ministry at Hope Conference and Renewal Center, Hope, N.J. He enjoys playing basketball and mountain biking, but doesn't have enough time to do either.

Emmy Lewis is from Lewisville, N.C. She is a graphic design major in the College of Design at North Carolina State University and will graduate spring of 2003. She is a youth leader at Raleigh (N.C.) Moravian Church and enjoys photography and reading.

Lindsay Moore is a junior at Davison (N.C.) College. She is currently studying art history and plans to pursue her studies in Florence, Italy, in the fall of 2001. She is a Young Life leader at Mooresville (N.C.) High School and is service chair at Connor Eating House.

Audrey Morgan currently resides in Bethlehem, Pa., and works at Mallinckrodt Baker, Inc., in Phillipsburg, N.J. She is a graduate of Salem College, Winston-Salem, N.C., with a dual major in economics and Spanish. Audrey says, "I have traveled and shared fellowship with Moravians in Tanzania, Honduras, and Costa Rica. These experiences have helped shape my world view and instilled in me a desire to work for the kingdom among various groups."

Chris New lives in Edmonton, Alberta, Canada—his hometown—with his wife, Aynsley and two small children. He is a pastor serving at Edmonton Moravian Church. Chris loves to play the piano and the organ whenever there's a spare moment. In 2001, he led a group of 23 Canadian youth to the Moravian Youth Convo' in Pennsylvania.

Melanie Perales is a digital designer in San Antonio, Texas, and is pursuing a degree in graphic arts. In addition to computers, Melanie enjoys singing, playing, and listening to music. She is one of six musicians in a contemporary Christian group called ana.

Mary Ridings, from Winston-Salem, N.C., is a student at Montreat College in Montreat, N.C. She is majoring in biblical studies and plans to go to seminary to become a minister.

The Rev. Tammie Rinker serves the Newfoundland Moravian Church, located in the Pocono region of Northeastern Pennsylvania. She is married to Ostomy Matthew and they have two children, Robert and Quinn. The family loves to garden, swim, ski, and worship together.

Beth Rohn currently resides in Lititz, Pa. She was recently installed as part of the pastoral staff of Lititz Moravian Church. A lifelong Moravian, she enjoys working with youth and counseling at church camps during the summer. She enjoys listening to several different types of music, but has been known to keep country and contemporary Christian music stations preset on her car radio. Her prayer is that all may know the power of the love of God.

Tamara Schoeneberger Lenig lives in Saylorsburg, Pa., with Andrew, her husband of nine years. Shortly after offering her life to Christ, music became predominant in her life. Recently, she has led worship for the congregation of her home church in Nazareth, Pa. She also keeps busy with other music ministries such as "Body Of Believers," a Saturday evening worship service, and the Christian rock band "oneWord." Blessed with gifts of piano, voice, and songwriting, she uses them all for the glory of God.